Recipes for prizewinning wines

by

BRYAN ACTON

ARGUS BOOK LIMITED

Published by

Amateur Winemaker Publications

Argus Books Limited
Wolsey House,
Wolsey Road,
Hemel Hempstead,
Herts. HP2 4SS,
England.

Cover by Cassedy Russell Design Consultants Ltd.

and line illustrations by STAN BAKER

First Impression: 1971
Second Impression: 1971
Third Impression: 1972
Fourth Impression: 1976
Fifth Impression: 1976
Sixth Impression: 1977
Seventh Impression: 1978
Eighth Impression: 1979
Ninth Impression: 1980
Eleventh Impression: 1981
Twelfth (enlarged) Impression: 1982
Thirteenth Impression 1984

SBN 900 841 16 8

Printed in Great Britain by
Standard Press (Andover) Ltd., South Street, Andover, Hampshire
Telephone: Andover 52413

CONTENTS

FRONTISPIECE

THE recipes in this book are mostly based upon prizewinning ones, and have been collected over many years. When a wine has won a major award at either a Regional show or the annual National, perhaps beating down eighty competitors, its recipe is obviously of value.

While, for a prizewinning wine, adequate maturation is required and always will be required, a great many wines can be drunk with satisfaction often within weeks only. This can only be done if the wine has been well compounded in the first place. Otherwise, immense time is needed to achieve a reasonable balance of smoothness.

If you are after prizewinning wines you will need to give them time to mature, but it is also true to say that a well-balanced wine will be drinkable long before one which is *not* well balanced and which was badly compounded in the first place.

The wines set out in this book, you will find, will both ferment and mature with astonishing rapidity because I have been at pains to ensure that ideal conditions are provided for yeast growth and activity, and thus for fermentation and quick maturation.

The additives used in this book for this purpose are simple ones obtainable from chemists and wine suppliers. Individually they have been recommended by many experts on winemaking. Combined, in the proportions advocated in this book's recipes, they will enable you to turn out quality wine—quickly.

In order to make this book complete in every sense, I have included a number of wines which are traditional or of historic interest and together they cover almost every class at the National Conference.

Happy winemaking,

Bryan Acton

It really is easy!

I could say that my four-year-old son David knows how to make wine. This is technically true, since as for my own daily use I make light wines, he knows that he only has to pour into a plastic bucket a can of fruit, two pounds of sugar and a teaspoonful from each of four jars I use, and then add the yeast and fill the bucket with water and we will in time have wine—not to his taste, of course, but as he says, "When I grow up I will probably like it."

This is how I suppose an experienced cook makes a cake, "a bit of this and a bit of that; slap it all in and you have a cake."

You can use this book in that way. The recipes give the method and include expertise about which you do not need to know the reason. There are some initial chapters about basic winemaking which are really to be read through from time to time. They are only a brief introduction to the art of winemaking. Still, if you make an outstanding wine, and I am sure you will, it is nice to be able to say how you did it. I hope that your successes will cause you to read more deeply into the subject.

Old time country wines were often excellent, but took from three to five years to clear and become drinkable. In the twentieth century we cannot afford this amount of time, at least I cannot. That is how this book was born, and to write it I explored the use of a few commercial wine techniques which can produce a wine which is clear and drinkable, at worst in months and at best in a matter of weeks. First of all get a drink and later on put some away for full maturing. This, by the way, does not apply to vegetable or grain wines. They still need time and no-one yet has found a short-cut to their speedy production.

If you are a beginner, start straight away with a trip to the super-market and get weaving on a recipe using canned fruit juice. Then work your way through the fruits and flowers, and leave the vegetables, grain and rhubarb until the finish. Make your wine in five-gallon lots, if you can, and put the top gallon of each five away for a two year period. This is the way to build an extensive cellar of quality wines.

THE NEW THINGS ABOUT WINEMAKING

In the old days only the very patient made wine. The conditions arranged for the poor yeast were so poverty stricken that only a small percentage of wines achieved any worthwhile quality, and these required several years of maturing to demonstrate it.

Conditions have changed. Peter Duncan and I, in writing our big book *Progressive Winemaking*, spent three years sifting through everything on wine we could find in English, French and German, and we backed this with experiments covering 900 gallons of wine. We naturally learned a lot about wine in this period. Mixtures of our native ingredients would balance up to the excellence of the grape and the careful balance of additives and would ensure a sound fermentation.

A further programme of experiments conducted with my friend the late Tom Henderson, Chairman of the Tunbridge Wells Circle, produced some remarkable results when Vitamin B was added to a fermentation.

The result of all this work was to spotlight about a dozen substances, mostly chemicals, which were large aids to winemaking. Of these only four are of vital importance, and no harder to obtain than a cook's equally essential salt, pepper, mustard and vinegar. They are all obtainable from either winemaking suppliers or from chemists who stock winemaking ingredients.

They are:

Vitamin B to ensure whatever alcohol strength you require within normal limits.

Ammonium Phosphate or Nutrient tablets to maintain sound fermentation.

Pectic Enzyme (Pectinol, pectolase, pectozyme, etc.), to speed up clarification of your wine.

Grape tannin or tannic acid as an essential adjustment to certain wines for flavour and character.

The use of these substances is explained later, along with some of the others which are mainly optional. The importance of these substances is that they aid you to jump from beginner to experienced winemaker in one great leap instead of over several years of steady progression.

A certain amount of the following is well known to established winemakers, but it is possible that you may have never made wine before in your life. It seems rather hard that you should be denied the joy of an unlimited supply of good wine at little cost. What follows then is a sort of instant winemaking course. It will steer you away from the errors of early winemaking, but please do not think that this is the whole of the art and science of winemaking. If it were, there would not be University courses on the subject in France and Germany.

HOW ONE MAKES WINE

Basically, one takes a solution consisting of fruit juice or an extraction of vegetables, flowers, herbs, etc., which provides a basic flavour and adds to it a certain amount of sugar which provides the alcohol required. Depending on the solution one then adds or does not need to add other things—tannin, acid nutrients, pectin clearing agents. This whole mixture is called the "must" and if the additions are correct it is an ideally balanced must equal to that provided by the best grapes. It is the ideal breeding ground for yeast, which is the true architect of the wine.

THE IMPORTANCE OF YEAST

Yeast is actually one of Nature's destruction agents. On a compost heap it is part of the process which reduced vegetable matter down to its basic elements so that life can once more rise from it. I never cease to wonder how with the special conditions we impose in winemaking, yeast produces alcohol, man's oldest joymaker and comfort in times of sorrow.

In the early stages of winemaking, we allow the yeast to behave as though it were on a compost heap. With plenty of air about it expands its colony at a fantastic rate, so that a tiny trace of a wine yeast culture becomes perhaps one million million yeast cells per gallon jar. Around this point the yeast will have used up the oxygen in the must. The yeast cell, however, is better adapted to survive than a human being. When we run out of air we die, but not the yeast cell. If it runs out of air it can still survive as long as there is some sugar about and the yeast has its normal food and growth factors provided by the must.

Under these conditions, the yeast obtains its energy from the sugar, and in doing so splits it into roughly equal weights of carbon dioxide gas and alcohol. Hundreds of other things happen also, giving the wine its final character, flavour and bouquet.

BASIC PROGRAMME OF MAKING A WINE

The whole business of making good wine is to abide by the laws of nature and to control them to one's own advantage. The basic sequence is as follows:

1. The juices are extracted and, generally, diluted with water.
2. Sugar, acid, tannin, nutrients, vitamins, etc., are added if necessary to produce a balanced "must".
3. The yeast is added, and with a reasonable supply of air, multiplies its colony rapidly.
4. The must is transferred to a jar, cutting off the air supply to the yeast, so that carbon dioxide gas and alcohol are formed.
5. Fermentation finishes when the sugar supply is exhausted, and the wine is siphoned into a fresh jar away from the yeast and pulp sediment.
6. Finally the wine is matured and bottled or drunk.

INGREDIENTS

It is difficult to be dogmatic about this, since there will always be someone who upsets the basic principles but still comes up with a magnificent wine.

Nevertheless, as a general rule, fruit of all sorts makes the best wines. Good wines can also be made from Grain, Flowers, Honey, Leaves and Shoots, but often more time is required for maturing. Vegetables, with few exceptions, are at the bottom of the list in terms of flavour.

Fresh ingredients are almost always better than dried. Perhaps the only exception to this rule is grape concentrate, which under its careful conditions of production, loses very little of its original quality. In this book, grape concentrate is used frequently as a balancing additive and even in small amounts is excellent for this purpose.

JUICE EXTRACTION

This is a very important stage of winemaking. Old books on country winemaking used methods of extracting the juice by either boiling the ingredients or pouring boiling water over it and then fermenting on the pulp for a few days, once it had cooled off. There are two disadvantages in this procedure as flavour is dissipated into the air by boiling, and, secondly, in some ingredients such as apricots, plums, etc., the pectin in the fruit is extracted which makes the later clearing of the wine a difficult task.

Even today, boiling or the use of boiling water, is still the best way of dealing with certain ingredients, but generally cold water extraction with safeguards is very much superior.

ADJUSTING THE MUST

In addition to the basic juice or extraction, some or all of the following are also needed to provide a balanced must:

Sugar
Acid
Nutrients and Growth factors
Pectic enzyme
Tannin

Let's have a look at each of these!

Sugar

There may be a certain amount of sugar in the juice already extracted. Grape concentrate is so rich in sugar that when it is used as the main ingredient it is often unnecessary to add any more. Dried fruits such as raisins often have half a pound of sugar per pound of raisins.

It is the total of sugar in the juice plus added sugar which decides the amount of alcohol which can be formed (up to the fermenting power of the yeast).

Very roughly, each pound of sugar dissolved in a gallon of must will provide about 5% alcohol by volume, or approximately 9 degrees of proof spirit. One pound per gallon is beer strength, two pounds per gallon is right for a table wine and three pounds per gallon is approaching a dessert wine.

It is not often advisable to have a higher amount of sugar per gallon than this. If, for instance, you put in four pounds per gallon it is probable that the yeast will only be able to ferment out three, leaving you with a very oversweet concoction which can hardly be called a wine. In case this has saddened you, let me reassure you that there is a special method of fermenting which often will allow you to obtain very high amounts of alcohol. This is outlined in the dessert wine section.

Always use ordinary white household sugar. Special sugars such as glucose, invert sugar, candy sugar, etc., are not necessary, and are certainly more expensive. Only in a few special cases are they superior. There are a few wines where Demerara sugar is useful because of its flavour.

ACIDS

Acids serve several valuable purposes. They inhibit hostile bacteria, aid fermentation on its normal course, become paramount during maturing, and finally influence the flavour of the finished wine. The acids we are concerned with are fruit acids of which there are at least 36 in wines. Only four of these are used in this book as adjustments and one other for maturing.

Acids

Citric Acid. This is the main acid in fruits such as oranges, currants, grapefruit, elderberries, strawberries, etc. It is liked for its flavour and does help promote a fast fermentation, but is of little use in maturing.

Malic Acid. This is the main acid in apples, apricots, blackberries, rhubarb, etc. It helps fermentation and is of great assistance during maturing. Although a prominent acid in the grape it is rarely used on its own because in excess it produces a somewhat sour flavour in the wine.

Tartaric Acid. This acid is found in quantity only in grapes and grape products (raisins, etc.). Grapes, because of their natural sugar contents are supreme for winemaking, and this, their main acid, imparts a flavour which makes it important, even though it is a poor fermenter and maturer.

Succinic Acid. Some of this acid will be in *all* your wines, being formed during fermentation. It is superior to all the previous acids in its ability to produce esters which give a wine its extra flavour and vinosity. To do it, however, it needs two years maturing, so keep it for your special wines.

Lactic Acid. This is an acid at last coming on the amateur winemaking market as this book goes to print. It is even superior to succinic acid, but is not normally used during fermentation. Had I known the supply position was resolved, it would have been built into almost every recipe. However, the secret is quite simple. Cut out half a teaspoonful (4 gms. or 1/7th oz.) of citric acid or malic acid in any recipe, ferment, and at the end of fermentation add one whole teaspoonful of 50% liquid lactic acid. Then keep it for two years. Then win prizes. Main distributor, Rogers Mead Ltd., 27 Vicarage Road, Wednesfield, Staffs., now available from most retailers.

VITAMIN B

It has been known for a long time that Vitamin B was an important growth factor for yeast. It is comparatively recently, however, that experiments done by myself and others have shown the great new potential opening up by using this vitamin regularly in every brew.

In a recent experiment I obtained 22% alcohol by volume (36 degrees proof) by direct fermentation. This brew, intended to be a dessert wine, was of course an attempt at perfection in alcohol production. It was based on grape concentrate and included all the additives recommended in this book. The Vitamin B cannot do the job on its own, but with a balanced must and suitable additives it does appear to achieve quite spectacular results.

I use a brand of Vitamin B1 called Benerva, obtainable through chemists. Tablets are obtainable cheaply, but do sell in various strengths from 3 mg. to 300 mg. The maximum dose per gallon of must is about 15 mg., so that you should obtain either 3 mg., 10 mg., or 25 mg. tablets (with the last named a tablet can easily be split into two). Winemakers overseas need to ask for tablets of aneurine hydrochloride or thiamine hydrochloride. Other brands of Vitamin B1 are suitable, of course, unless they have a base of brewers yeast. There have not been enough experiments yet to discover whether a beery taste is imparted to the wine.

Other vitamins may also assist the fermentation—for instance the riboflavin and nicotinamide constituents of the whole Vitamin B complex. Thus a Benerva Compound tablet can be used if straight Vitamin B1 is unobtainable.

In an emergency, with no tablets around, use a quarter of a teaspoonful of Marmite per gallon, which will assist matters considerably.

NUTRIENTS:
AMMONIUM SALTS

These are important as a source of nitrogen, required by the yeast. They are in general the main ingredient in nutrient tablets supplied to winemakers. I personally use Ammonium Phosphate and buy it from chemists in 500 gram jars. This lasts for a hundred gallons, I suppose. For novices it is probable that a tube of nutrient tablets from any winemaking supplier is more satisfactory.

POTASSIUM PHOSPHATE

Potassium is an essential growth factor, but most ingredients contain enough of it. As such it is an optional additive. It does no harm to add it and in some cases proves important.

MAGNESIUM SULPHATE (EPSOM SALTS)

This is a trace element, absolutely essential to a good fermentation. A must which lacks magnesium is alike a human body without vitamins or a garden deficient of boron. Nothing really grows very well. As before, a lot of ingredients contain enough magnesium, otherwise the amateur winemaking movement would never have got going, and fermentations would be sticking all over the place. It really depends on your water supply. If you live in Birmingham or Glasgow, for example, you have no need to add this to your must. Things are not quite so good in London, Liverpool and Cardiff. A small pinch per gallon is all that is needed, or a phone call to your local Water Board to find out the position.

PECTIN

The stuff which makes natural jams set solid is pectin. It is a hazard to winemaking, causing persistent hazes. Fortunately we have available pectin-destroying enzymes which chop the pectin molecules to bits and produce clear wines.

They are sold at present under trade names of Pectinol, Pectolase, etc. They work about twenty times better when there is no alcohol present, and so a teaspoonful per gallon put in at the same time as the yeast works wonders. It is important to put them in with the yeast, for, like the yeast, they cannot stand extremes of heat.

They can also be used to clear finished wines which are hazy due to pectin, but larger quantities are required.

12

I have so got into the habit of using one or other of the above products that I put it in even when I know there cannot be any pectin present. It's a good habit to get into.

TANNIN

Tannin is a minor but very important constituent of wine. Its effect is to produce a certain bite on the palate which is desirable in red wines (which are rich in tannin) and it also acts as a protective agent and assists clarification of wines.

Most true red wines such as red grape, elderberry, etc,, are rich in tannin as are white wines made from apples or pears. Some red wines, such as blackberry or beetroot, are not true red wines and require tannin additions. Excess tannin, as occurs occasionally in elderberries, can be removed with a fining agent such as egg white.

The three main sources of tannin are grape tannin (from a wine-maker supplier), tannic acid (from a chemist) or cold tea. Their order of preference is as stated and cold tea should only be used in an emergency, half a cup of strong tea replacing the dosage in the recipe.

CHOICE OF YEASTS

To be a good winemaker you think about your yeast. Most novices think about the main ingredient and this is wrong. If the yeast is happy and healthy then a good wine can be made from practically anything of vegetable origin, and even from animal substances such as honey or milk. One looks after one's yeast as though it were one's faithful cat or dog.

You start with a pedigree yeast—a wine yeast. These are now plentiful from winemaking suppliers, and come in all varieties of commercial wines in either liquid or dried form. While acknowledging that the dried varieties are now much better than they once were, I still prefer the liquid cultures. Do not fall into the error of thinking that if you buy, say, a Sauternes yeast and use it with parsnips that you are going to make Sauternes. The truth of the matter is that if you prepare a mixture of ingredients which produce a sort of Sauternes wine, anyway, the Sauternes yeast will add that little extra in the same direction.

My own general choice of varieties—it is my own and someone may well have different ideas—is:

Dry Red wines: Burgundy or Bordeaux

Dry White wines: Bordeaux, Zeltinger or Burgundy
Sweet Red wines: Madeira or Port
Sweet White wines: Sauternes or Tokay

In any case, a wine yeast of any sort is preferable to baker's yeast. You can make good wines with baker's yeast, but if you have failure it is most likely to be a failure where your wine tastes of bread. Similarly, the use of brewers yeast will produce wines tasting like beer.

YEAST STARTERS

If you buy a wine yeast you will either use a single tablet or tiny sachet of yeast or a liquid culture with a tiny smear of yeast. This is in fact enough to start off a gallon of must, but since the yeast must dominate the must to squeeze out the hostile bacteria, it is better to build it up somewhat.

What we normally do is to use the culture to make a wine bottleful of fermenting must and use this as a starter for a gallon of wine. A gallon of fermenting must is in turn a starter for a ten gallon brew, and a ten gallon brew is a good starter for a hundred gallon cask if your living room is so big.

The following is not the ideal yeast starter as described in *Progressive Winemaking*, but I have only found it to fail in two cases in my last hundred brews. The risks are worth it for a beginner, since the process is so simple.

Method

Take a wine bottle and wash it out with both hot and cold water. Wash out a funnel in like manner, and dry it. Put into the bottle through the funnel a level dessertspoonful of sugar (an American tablespoonful), the juice of a large orange, a 3 mg. Vitamin B tablet, and top up to the shoulder with cold tap water. Mix well and add the yeast tablet or culture and plug the bottle with cotton wool. Stand in a temperature of 75°F. (24°C).

After 24 hours, give the bottle a gentle shake and tip it slightly on one side. When a stream of bubbles flow up the side you can start making your wine.

I admitted earlier that this method has its occasional failure. With liquid yeast cultures I have never yet found it to fail. It has failed with dried yeasts, but these are so much cheaper than liquid cultures that nothing really has been lost. You just start again since your main ingredients have not yet been committed to the must.

CONTINUATION OF FERMENTATION

Once the yeast starter is going well, the must is prepared as per recipe and eventually finishes in a bubbling gallon jar or carboy.

All you have to do now is to let Nature take its course. The beginner finds difficulty here in that after the first violent fermentation the wine must settles down to a steady bubbling and it is difficult to decide when fermentation is sufficiently finished to terminate it. The ideal way is with the hydrometer, so read the hydrometer chapter which follows. This is not unduly scientific. Most motorists use a hydrometer to test the liquid in their batteries; it is a very simple device and to my mind the most important piece of winemaking equipment I use. I can manage without most of the gadgetry of winemaking, but without a hydrometer I would be lost.

If you do not want to use a hydrometer then you must rely on your palate to decide when most of the sugar has been taken out of the must. The point is roughly this: if you have a light table wine fermenting, with about two pounds of sugar per gallon only, it should ferment out to finishing point in about three weeks at 75°F. (24°C). At this point something over 10% alcohol will have been formed. The must will in fact continue fermenting at a very slow rate for perhaps three months further, and in that time will only add perhaps half of one per cent to the ten already formed. There is no point in tying up jars for this long period for such tiny additional alcohol, and a great risk is run if pulp in the jar starts to disintegrate.

It is important, therefore, to find the finishing point satisfactory to you, kill off the remaining fermentation and remove the wine from its yeast and pulp deposit. This is done by adding one Campden tablet per gallon, which stuns the yeast, and racking (siphoning) the wine off into a fresh jar a few days later.

After this the second jar is topped up with *water* and a bored cork plugged with cotton wool is fitted (or an air-lock) and the wine merely has to mature before drinking or bottling. Do not make the common mistake of beginners of topping up the second jar with sugar syrup, in the hope of getting a bit more alcohol. This tends to cause a weak fermentation which can continue for years, produces little additional alcohol, and merely prevents the wine from clearing.

MATURING

This is a simple matter. Some wines are ready to drink only a few weeks after the termination of fermentation. Others require perhaps one or two years' maturation. The latter need to be stored in cool surroundings (though this is not critical with our robust country wines) and small additions of air are required every four months. This is achieved by pouring the wine from one jar to another and topping up the second jar with water exactly as at the first racking. The yeast deposit is by now fairly firm and will not come over into the second jar. The little which does tends to act as a fining agent and helps produce a star-bright wine.

HYDROMETER

I have already stressed the importance of the hydrometer. It is simply a weighted and very fragile bulb with a graduated tube above it. It floats in wine in a cylindrical tube called a trial jar. Most winemaking suppliers sell these and they are not expensive, provided you treat them as very fragile, i.e. always hold them upright and never let them drop into a jar.

The hydrometer has several uses in determining how much alcohol is likely to be achieved in wine, but in this book its principal function is to determine the point at which fermentation can be considered to have finished.

A practical example is perhaps the best way to illustrate this: let us suppose you are making a full-bodied parsnip wine, using four pounds of parsnips and three pounds of sugar as the main ingredients. At the start of fermentation the hydrometer will register about 110 (known as a gravity of 110). This actually indicates a potential alcohol of over 15%. As fermentation proceeds, subsequent tests show lower readings, as the alcohol builds up (alcohol is lighter than water). Eventually the hydrometer almost disappears in the trial jar of wine, or at least goes down to the 1000 mark (zero gravity) and this indicates the wine is sufficiently finished to terminate fermentation. If one wanted a very dry wine, one might let it ferment on a bit further, but with, say, parsnip, which is hardly ever drunk as a dry wine, and with 15% alcohol formed and a kick like a horse, one would terminate the fermentation and sweeten it up later when it is more mature. The method of killing off the yeast is explained in the following section under Sulphite.

SULPHITE

This is not a strange substance to you. Look in your larder and you will find all sorts of things, such as fruit squashes, preserves, etc., which list either Sodium Metabisulphite, Sulphite or Sulphur Dioxide among their ingredients on the can or bottle. It is a safe preservative, used for many years, which has never fallen under suspicion of being harmful to human beings in the quantities used by winemakers.

Winemakers buy sulphite in the form of Campden tablets from chemists or winemaking suppliers and each tablet is equal to 50 parts per million sulphur dioxide in a gallon. It is cheaper to buy the chemical as sodium metabisulphite in 500 gm. lots and to make up a stock solution by dissolving this quantity in a gallon of water. Five mls. of this powerful solution is equal to a Campden tablet, and a pint of it can be used over and over again to sterilise jars until it loses its smell. If using this powerful solution it is important not to inhale the fumes since they will produce a choking effect.

Campden tablets or sulphite are mainly used in four ways:
1. When preparing the must, when boiling water is not used to sterilise ingredients, one Campden tablet per gallon will kill off most hostile bacteria while not affecting the yeast, although a 24 hour wait is advisable before adding the yeast.
2. At the end of fermentation, one Campden tablet per gallon added to the must will stun the remaining yeast and this tends to sink to the bottom of the jar bringing down bits of pulp with it, thus allowing the wine to be racked off a few days later into a fresh jar.
3. At all rackings, the addition of one Campden tablet per gallon will prevent damage to the wine by excessive oxygen reaching it during racking. This is mainly important with white wines.
4. A separate solution of a dozen Campden tablets dissolved in a pint of water is a useful antiseptic to disinfect jars and bottles. The solution is simply poured into the jar, the jar swirled round to wash its interior with the solution, and the solution then poured back into its container.

Over a period of time the solution will become discoloured, but is still effective as long as a *very careful* sniff indicates it retains its pungent smell.

ACID TESTING

I once overheard a winemaker say to another: "You have to be a fanatic if you test the acid in your wines." This is probably true if wine is made in single gallons, and you are not expected to do it in this book except perhaps in a recipe here and there in the prize-winning section.

It is much easier, of course, to make wine in five or ten gallon lots than in single gallons. Less time is consumed in the effort, but with such a quantity the level of acid becomes important and it is as well to test it.

Since you do not need this knowledge with this book, but are likely to do so once you start filling the house with liquor, I will just briefly explain the system.

There are two ways of looking at acid. The first is the total amount of acid present, which is measured by titration. The most accurate method of determining this is as described in *Progressive Winemaking*, but involves acquiring a little bit of equipment—burette, pipette and solutions of caustic soda and phenolphthalein. There is a simpler and cheaper testing kit sold by the winemaking supplier Loftus. The latter, while not intended to be as accurate as the standard laboratory equipment, is perfectly adequate if used with care, and it also includes tests for pectin and starch hazes.

Determining the total amount of acid present ensures that there is enough for satisfactory fermentation and gives a close idea of the amount needed for the finished wine.

The second aspect of acid is what is called its pH value. It to some extent represents the active part of the acid which makes a wine taste acid or not. Ideally it is tested with a pH meter, but these are so expensive and messy to use that only a few dedicated winemakers have them. There are, however, pH papers which are torn out of a tiny book and dipped in the wine, the resultant colour change being compared with a standard. A pH figure of 3.2 is the ideal for a great many wines. If it is lower than this it is too acid, if higher, acid generally needs to be added.

When I am inventing new recipes I use both methods, but then I cannot afford a bad recipe getting into print. You would write me letters in varying heights of dudgeon depending on the amount you made.

NEW MEASURES

It is encouraging that the amateur winemaking movement which started in Andover has grown into a world-wide movement. They make wine in Moscow as in London, just south of Mount Everest and in Japan, and they read the *Amateur Winemaker*. It is necessary therefore to cater in weights and volumes for both the English system and the Metric sytem. A further complication arises from the growing winemaking movement in the United States. In the States they have gallons only four-fifths the size of the British ones, and tablespoons equal to British dessertspoons. We still more or less speak the same language, but I would appreciate letters from the USA from readers who find English ingredients have different names in their particular State.

The recipes are designed for each system and are not always straight conversions from one system to another. If a recipe states a teaspoonful of something in the USA column it is an American teaspoon which, like the gallon, is only four-fifths the size of a British one.

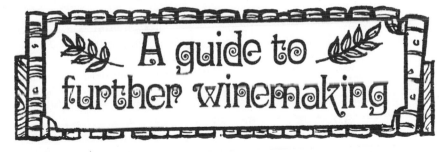

This book is of course mainly a recipe book, with just enough technical information to avoid any catastrophes. Winemaking is a vast subject, and university courses exist on the Continent as an adjunct to the commercial wine world.

It is a fascinating craft and one never tires of it, quite apart from the end product. The greatest moments are when you go to you little den, surrounded by casks, jars and bottles and pour yourself a drink. It is then that you sit back and say "Now, what shall I do next?" There are so many interesting things to do, but they require more knowledge than is contained in this book. As in all these matters there is generally a short-cut. The pioneers have made the mistakes and learnt the lessons and now there is a clear-cut road to success if only it can be found. I am suggesting her one such path to guide you.

NOVICES STAGE

Here you need to acquire equipment, mainly gallon jars and the few basic acids, nutrients, etc., needed for brews. Avoid gadgets at this stage other than a few fermentation locks (air-locks). Try and get a copy of the WINEMAKER (*Amateur Winemaker and Home Brewer*) from your local bookstall. It is a monthly, full of interesting articles, but at this stage more important for sources of supply of ingredients, particularly in winter. A paperback, *First Steps in Winemaking*, is also very useful to fill in the basic knowledge of winemaking.

INTERMEDIATE STAGE

You have by now got a few gallons resting and should start making wine in five gallon lots. Make it in fives, rack it off into single gallon jars and put one of these away for full maturing. The cellar of class wines is now in the making. You will probably want to simulate commercial wines such as Burgundy, Claret, Sauternes, Port and Sherry. The recipes for these type of wines are in a paperback called *Making Wines Like those you Buy*.

LATE INTERMEDIATE STAGE

This is a tricky stage. You have some good wines coming on, but information is coming in so fast that it is difficult to absorb it.

This is the time to join a wine circle. There are hundreds of these all over the country, all very friendly, and you do not have to feel rotten if you have no good wines to bring along. Make sure you bring a glass, for someone will give you a drink. Take along a bottle of unfinished wine for an opinion. It starts a conversation and you will soon feel at home and unravel the problems of this stage. Every circle has talks, films, competitions, barbecues, outings and general binges. Every circle has its full quota of shy people, steady drinkers and outrageous types. We all feel quite at home!

ADVANCED STAGE

This is the stage of the specialist. You may want to concentrate on making a particular type of wine or just be better than everyone

20

else. It is really a question of reading and experiment. The following check-list of additional books will help you:

Advanced Books

Progressive Winemaking—the standard textbook on every aspect of winemaking.

Modern Winemaking Techniques—This book details the methods of juice extraction, and how to obtain the best results from a wider range of ingredients.

Scientific Winemaking Made Easy—informative, readable and scientific.

Whys and Wherefores of Winemaking—a compendium of useful background information.

Recipe Books

Amateur Winemaking Recipes and *130 New Winemaking Recipes*—recipes for the lovers of country wines.

Beer

All About Beer, Brewing Better Beers, Home Brewed Beers and Stouts and *Brewing Beers Like Those You Buy*—Well tried recipes for beers and methods of beer-making.

All the Year Round Winemaking

Making Wine with Canned and Dried Fruit

Miscellaneous

Making Mead—a treatise on the world's oldest wine with recipes for wines such as Julius Caesar or Good Queen Bess would have drunk. Chapter 2 is for those feeling a bit low.

Growing Vines—how to start your own vineyard.

Making Cider—The only book currently available on this fascinating and ultra-British craft. Recipes for sweet, dry, still and sparkling cider, and cider cookery.

Be a Wine and Beer Judge—an authoritative guide for both judges and those entering wines in competitions.

All the books quoted in this Chapter are obtainable as paper backs from Argus Books Ltd., Wolsey House, Wolsey Road, Hemel Hempstead, Herts. HP2 4SS. Send for price list.

Assuming you have just picked up this book and have never made wine before, I have to ensure, in a practical way, that you will become one of that happy crowd of winemakers who always have a drink about the house when friends call. So let me describe to you how to make the simplest of wines, which is practically foolproof and will produce a *vin-ordinaire*. It is not a great wine, but is intended to be up to the standard of the cheaper commercial wines of its type and to be drunk in a few weeks time. Its cost per bottle is about one-tenth of its commercial equivalent. In making it, by obtaining the supporting additives you are already stocking up your wine larder for future brews.

YOU NEED

1 pint of canned orange juice
2 lb. of sugar
These, of course, come from a supermarket.
2 jars of 1 gallon capacity. Alternatively you can often obtain half gallon jars from chemists and split the brew. Gallon jars are obtained from winemaking suppliers, off-licences and pubs.
1 yard of plastic tubing and a siphon tube. (Winemaking suppliers and chemists supply these, but they are not needed for a couple of weeks.)

Additives
A wine yeast (Bordeaux, Burgundy, Hock, General purpose)
Pectic enzyme (Pecintol, Pectolase, etc.)
Nutrient tablets (these replace Ammonium Phosphate in recipes)
Vitamin B1 (such as Benerva 3 mg. tablets from any chemist)
Campden tablets
The yeast, pectic enzyme, nutrients tablets and Campden tablets

can only be obtained from those chemists which stock winemaking supplies or from a winemaking supplier. There may be one of the latter in your district, but as it is your first brew I am listing the addresses of a few major suppliers who deal with mail-order business. I list these particular ones since they just happen to be my main suppliers over the years, and I have not had any reason for complaint either in quality or speed of delivery. I suggest you write off for their price lists.

Joseph Bryant Ltd.,
Broad Plain,
Bristol.

Continental Wine Experts Ltd.,
The Winery, Cawston,
Norfolk NR10 4BQ.

W. R. Loftus Ltd.,
16 The Terrace,
Torquay, Devon

Leigh-Williams & Sons,
Tattenhall,
Nr. Chester CH3 9PT.

Southern Vinyards Ltd.,
Nizells Avenue, Hove,
E. Sussex BN3 1PS

Roger Mead Ltd.,
Shirlett, Broseley,
Salop. TF12 5BH.

Vina Ltd.,
Hornby Boulevard,
Bootle, Liverpool L20 5HP

Method

Having got all the above, wash out the gallon jar thoroughly. Next, sterilise the jar by crushing a couple of Campden tablets and putting them in the jar with about a cupful of water. Carefully swill this liquid all over the inside of the jar for about a minute. This will kill off hostile bacteria. Then empty out the liquid and once more wash the jar out with cold water.

Pour into the jar all the ingredients, first the solid ones and then the liquid ones, say, in this order:

2 lb. sugar, 1 nutrient tablet (crushed)
1 Benerva tablet (3 mg.) (crushed)
1 level teaspoon Pectic enzyme 1 pint orange juice

Now add *cold* water up to shoulder of jar and mix everything well to dissolve solids. Then add yeast and plug the top of the jar with a big wad of cotton wool to keep out insects. Keep in a warm room temperature of about 70°–75°F. (21°–24°C.). Under these conditions the jar should be fermenting in about 36 hours. I have taken one or two risks with this recipe in order not to complicate matters, but the chances of failure are very small. Once the jar is fermenting, leave it alone for at least a fortnight. The gas coming off is protecting the wine against hostile forces. After about two weeks you will see that the bubbling has died down and the fermenting wine can be tasted to see if most of the sugar has been turned into alcohol. The jar can now be topped up to the neck with cold water.

After about one more week, depending on temperature, the wine should be ready for racking (siphoning away from the yeast sediment). It may still be bubbling lightly, but on tasting it should appear very dry and possibly unpalatable. Expect the latter at this stage.

Now add one crushed Campden tablet to the wine, stir the jar a little and leave it for four days, replacing the cotton wool plug.

Next lift the jar carefully on to a table and place the clean secon. gallon jar on the floor. Put the siphon tube gently in the jar and suck on the plastic tube attached to it so that the wine siphons down into the second jar. Do not tip the first jar to get the last drop out of it or you will defeat your purpose which is to get the wine away from the sediment. Top up the second jar with cold water and preferably fit a bored cork plugged with cotton wool. Cover it, anyway, to keep out insects.

Leave the wine for three weeks, siphon it once more into the first jar, and then taste it. It is most probable that you will not like so dry a taste. Sweeten it up therefore by first making a syrup. One pound of sugar is boiled up with half a pint of water, and an addition of one teaspoonful of citric or tartaric acid (from any chemist) is desirable, as a little more acid is needed to balance the extra sugar. When the syrup is cool, first add a quarter of a pint of this syrup to the wine, mix it in well and taste again. If this is all right fill your decanters with the wine and drink it. If not, sweeten it further.

It is a light *vin-ordinaire* meant to be drunk as a dry wine or a medium dry one. You can make much better wines later. It is, however, the first stage in the lead-up to the point where you can look worried and exclaim, "I am down to my last fifty gallons—I shall have to get cracking!"

Preparing wines for exhibition

Many good winemakers slip up when it comes to showing. They do not read the show schedule which lays down the rules of the game they are playing. Many other good winemakers, having won a prize with a wine, suffer mental lapses at this point in the joy of their success. They take their winning bottle home, top it up with some more of the same wine and enter it in another show only a week later, when it fails dismally. What has been forgotten is that the wine (on its winning run) has been tasted, and thus a partly full bottle has been exposed to the air for many hours, possibly in a hot marquee tent. The air and the heat have started millions of chemical reactions which may or may not improve the wine. Even if this burst of oxygen proves beneficial, it requires several more weeks in bottle to achieve this.

We of the National Guild of Judges are sinned against much more than we sin when it comes to wine judging. All the same, in the interests of friendly relations between the Guild and the competitors, the following hints may well help you to get that coveted cup.

SHOW SCHEDULE

When you enter a show, you are sent a show schedule. Please read it carefully and read it again when you are getting your bottles ready for the show. It will generally specify the type of bottle and cork, where the label should be fixed and even the amount of space required between the wine and the cork. If you fail to comply with these rules you may lose marks, or in extreme cases have your beautiful wine disqualified before it has been tasted.

PREPARING THE BOTTLE

According to most show schedules, you start with a clean, unscratched, white punted wine bottle and a cork of the type specified. From now on you must consider the various points of judging at which marks can be won or lost.

Presentation (2 points)

Points are lost if the wrong bottle is used, if it is scratched or dirty, if the cork is the wrong type, or if the level of wine in the bottle is incorrect. Points are also lost if the label is in the wrong position.

Clarity and Colour (4 points)

The ideal wine is star-bright, in that a lighted candle can be seen through the bottle without any sensation of haze. If, however, your wine is clear but not quite brilliant, it is better to leave it so rather than resort to any sort of filtering process, which may well impair the flavour where more marks are at stake. Colour, by the way, only occupies one mark in this section and should not be worried about unduly.

Bouquet (4 points)

Speaking loosely, about half the bouquet comes from the ingredient and half from the maturing. If, therefore, you were able to enter a couple of bottles in any class, then the chances are that an apple wine would have a better bouquet than a parsnip wine (wines of the same age) and a five year old apple wine would have a better bouquet than a one year old one (both matured under ideal conditions). Fruit generally has an advantage over vegetables due to its natural bouquet, and age has an advantage over youth due to the added bouquet formed during maturing.

Flavour (20 points)

Here are two-thirds of the available points and the flavour you have must be preserved.

DANGERS TO AVOID

Hazard No. 1. Danger of sediment being sucked into the show bottle.

Cure. Try and take your show bottleful from at least a half gallon jar and keep the siphon tube well above the sediment. Also wash the siphon tube before use in case it is at all dusty.

Hazard No. 2. Danger of oxidation.

Cure. Keep the level of the jar and the bottle close to each other so that siphoning is slow and without splashing. Keep the end of the tube in the bottle down at the bottom of the bottle for the same reason.

Hazard No. 3. Start of chemical reaction causing bottle sickness.

Cure. Prepare your show bottles, if possible, one month before the show so that everything will have stabilised itself once more and possibly even have improved the wine.

Some notes on Flower Wines

SPECIAL NOTES

Frequently flowers are used in wines either on their own, or as additives in order to provide additional bouquet. Quite often the flowers are out of season at the time the winemaker wishes to make his wine, so either dried flowers can be purchased from herbalists or health food shops, or many winemakers do in fact dry their own flowers for use out of season. The following tables gives an approximate equivalent of the amount of dried flowers required to be used to replace the normal amount of fresh flowers.

Dried Dandelions	1 oz. = 4 pint fresh = 2¼ litres
Dried Rose Petals	1 oz. = 5 pints fresh = 2¾ litres
Dried Elderflowers	1 oz. = 8 pints fresh = 4½ litres
Dried Cowslips	1 oz. = 2½ pints fresh = 1½ litres
Dried Rose hip shells	1 oz. = ½ lb. fresh = 227 gm.
Dried Coltsfoot	1 oz. = 4 pints fresh = 2¼ litres
Dried Parsley	1 oz. = ½ lb. fresh = 227 gm.

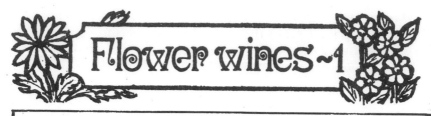

Flower wines ~1

HAWTHORN BLOSSOM WINE (MAYBLOSSOM)

Ingredients:	British	Metric	U.S.A
Hawthorn Blossoms	2 quarts	2 litres	3 pints
Sugar	2 lb.	1 kg.	1¾ lb.
White grape concentrate	½ pint	¼ litre	½ pint

Yeast—preferably white wine variety
Additives as above
Water to 1 gallon (4½ litres)

Method: Put the Hawthorn blossom in a plastic bucket, along with the sugar, grape concentrate and additives above. Pour on 6 pints (3 litres) of cold water. Stir thoroughly to dissolve sugar, etc. Add 1 Campden tablet (50 p.p.m. sulphite) and cover. Leave for 24 hours. After 24 hours add an active yeast, and ferment on the flowers for 4 days at a temperature of approximately 70°F. (21°C.). Strain the liquid off the flowers into a gallon jar, and fit a bored cork with an airlock plugged with cotton wool. Raise the temperature if possible to 75°F. (24°C.). Ferment to dryness, i.e. the gravity should fall below the zero mark. Rack into a fresh jar, and top up with water if necessary, add 1 Campden tablet and fit a bored cork tightly plugged with cotton wool. This wine becomes drinkable after a few weeks, but improves with maturing up to 2 years. It requires sweetening with up to ½ lb. sugar per gallon (225 gm. metric—6 oz. U.S.A.).

ELDERFLOWER WINE

Ingredients and method as for Hawthorn Blossom wine, except that only 1 pint of flowers per gallon is required (½ litre metric, ¾ pint U.S.A.). It is important that white flowers are picked in preference to the heavy clusters of creamy yellow ones, as the latter tend to give a "catty" flavour to the wine.

DANDELION WINE

Ingredients and method as for Hawthorn Blossom wine, except that 2 quarts of dandelion flowers are required (2 litres metric, 3 pints U.S.A.). No green parts should be included as these impart bitterness.

COWSLIP WINE

Ingredients and method as for Hawthorn Blossom wine, except that 1 gallon of flowers are required (4½ litres metric, 1 gallon U.S.A.). It is possible to make this wine with half the amount of flowers, but in this case the grape concentrate should be fermented for 4 days in the bucket and the flowers added for a further 4 days once the first heady fermentation has died down. The fermentation temperature should also be kept down to 65°–70°F. (18°–21°C.) only. This means a longer fermentation but helps preserve the delicate bouquet of these flowers.

COLTSFOOT WINE

Ingredients and method as for Hawthorn Blossom wine, except that 1 gallon coltsfoot flowers are required (4½ litres) metric, 1 gallon U.S.A.).

CLOVER WINE

Ingredients and method as for Hawthorn Blossom wine, except that 1 gallon flowers are required (4½ litres metric, 1 gallon U.S.A.). If pink clover is used, the finished wine will be a delicate rosé colour.

Flower wines ~2

ADDITIVES FOR 1 GALLON (4½ litres)

Essential   12 mg. Benerva (Vitamin B1 tablets)
1 heaped teaspoon citric acid (7 gm.)
¼ oz. tartaric acid (7 gm.)
½ teaspoon grape tannin or tannic acid
1 teaspoon ammonium phosphate or 1 nutrient tablet

Advisable 1 teaspoon Pectinol, Pectolase

Optional ½ teaspoon potassium phosphate
¼ teaspoon Epsom salts (if local water deficient in magnesium)
⅛ oz. succinic acid (if maturing wine for 2 years) (3 gm.)

PRIMROSE WINE

Ingredients:	British	Metric	U.S.A
Primrose petals	2 quarts	2 litres	3 pints
Sugar	2 lb.	1 kg.	1¾ lb.
White grape concentrate	½ pint	¼ litre	½ pint

Wine yeast—Champagne, Hock or Bordeaux
Additives as above
Water to 1 gallon (4½ litres)

Method: Put the primroses in a plastic bucket, along with the sugar, grape concentrate and additives above. Pour on 6 pints of cold water. Stir thoroughly to dissolve sugar, etc. Add 1 Campden tablet (50 p.p.m. sulphite) and cover. Leave for 24 hours. After 24 hours add an active yeast, and ferment on the flowers for 4 days at a temperature of approximately 70°F. (21°C.). Strain the liquid on the flowers into a gallon jar, and fit a bored cork with an airlock plugged with cotton wool. Raise the temperature, if possible, to 75°F. (24°C.). Ferment to dryness, i.e. the gravity should fall below the zero mark. Rack into a fresh jar, and top up with water, if necessary, add 1 Campden tablet, fit a bored cork tightly plugged with cotton wool. This wine becomes drinkable after a few weeks, but improves with maturing up to 2 years. The wine requires sweetening with up to ½ lb. sugar per gallon (225 gm. metric— 6 oz. U.S.A.).

AGRIMONY WINE
Ingredients: 1 medium sized bunch of agrimony
Otherwise recipe is exactly as for Primrose wine. In view of the flavour of agrimony, it is advisable to make this wine into a sweet wine, by the addition of just over ¼ lb. sugar per gallon once the wine has become stable.

GORSE WINE
Ingredients: 1 gallon of gorse flowers (4½ litres)
2½ lb. sugar per gallon (1 kg. metric—1 lb. U.S.A.)
Otherwise the recipe is exactly as for Primrose wine. It is advisable to collect flowers with a pair of gloves in view of the prickly nature of this plant.

GOLDEN ROD WINE
Ingredients: 2 handfuls Golden Rod petals
Otherwise the recipe is exactly as for Primrose wine. This wine has a particular flavour which requires muting, and therefore it is advisable to mature it for at least one year.

MARIGOLD WINE
Ingredients: 1 gallon of marigold flowers (4½ litres)
Otherwise the recipe is exactly as for Primrose wine. Like Golden Rod wine this flavour is particularly pungent, and therefore requires at least one year's maturing to bring it to its best.

PANSY WINE
Ingredients: 1 gallon of pansy petals (4½ litres)
Otherwise this recipe is exactly as for Primrose wine.

ROSE PETAL WINE
Ingredients: 2 quarts of rose petals (2 litres)
Otherwise this wine is exactly as for Primrose wine. It should be mentioned here that if red petals are used the final colour of the wine will be a light rosé colour, so that for a white wine only white or yellow petals should be used.

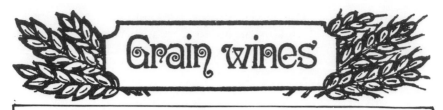

Grain wines

⊁ADDITIVES FOR 1 GALLON (4½ litres)

Essential   12 mg. Benerva (Vitamin B tablets)
¼ oz. malic acid (7 gm.)
¼ oz. citric acid (7 gm.)
¼ oz. tartaric acid (7 gm.)
½ teaspoon grape tannin or tannic acid
1 teaspoon ammonium phosphate or 1 nutrient
tablet

Advisable 1 teaspoon Amylozyme 100 (from winemaking
suppliers)
½ teaspoon potassium phosphate
¼ teaspoon Epsom salts (if local water deficient
in magnesium)
⅛ oz. succinic acid (if maturing wine for 2 years)
(3 gm.)

BARLEY WINE

Ingredients:	*British*	*Metric*	*U.S.A*
Pearl Barley	1 lb.	450 gm.	¾ lb.
White grape concentrate	½ pint	300 mls.	½ pint
Sugar	3 lb.	1400 gm.	2½ lb.

Any wine yeast
Additives as above
Water to 1 gallon (4½ litres)

Method: Put barley and sugar in a plastic bucket, and pour over 6 pints of boiling water. Stir to dissolve sugar. When cooled to room temperature 70°F. (21°C.), add grape concentrate and additives as above. Stir well to dissolve acids, and add active yeast starter. Cover and ferment on barley for 6 days. Strain liquor off barley into a gallon jar, fit a bored cork with cotton wool or an airlock. Ferment to dryness. With this wine this will be around 0–6° gravity. Rack into another jar, add 1 Campden tablet, and top up with cold water.

Fit a bored cork plugged with cotton wool. Mature for up to 18 months with rackings at 6-month intervals. Once wine is stable it may require further sweetening in order to balance the body and high alcohol content of this wine. It should be pointed out that this wine has a "kick" which also has a delayed action. This is definitely not a wine to be drunk if one is going to drive.

MAIZE WINE
Ingredients: 1½ lb. maize (680 gm. metric—1¼ lb. U.S.A.) replaces Barley
Otherwise ingredients and method as for Barley wine.

MALT WINE
Ingredients: 2 lb. malt extract (900 gm. metric, 1½ lb. U.S.A.) replaces Barley.
Remaining ingredients as for Barley Wine. Since malt extract is a heavy liquid, there is no need for pulp fermentation, and the ingredients can be mixed with lukewarm water direct into the gallon jar. However, the yeast and the Amylozyme 100 should not be put in until the temperature has gone down to room temperature. Otherwise the recipe is as for Barley wine.

RICE WINE
Ingredients: 3 lb. (1.4 kg. metric—2½ lb. U.S.A.) replaces Barley. Husked rice is better than polished rice.
Otherwise the recipe is exactly as for Barley wine.

WHEAT WINE
Ingredients: 1 pint wheat (½ litre metric—¾ pint U.S.A.) replaces Barley.
Otherwise the recipe is exactly as for Barley wine.

FURTHER VARIATIONS
Interesting variations of straight grain wines can be made by the addition of citrus fruits, or by flowers. For instance, the addition of the juice of 1 large grapefruit produces a barley and grapefruit wine which is an interesting aperitif. The addition of 1 packet of dried lime flowers makes an attractive wine with a bouquet normally absent from grain wines. Similarly other additions such as the juice of a large Jaffa orange can be added to produce changes from a normal straight grain wine.

Wines from leaves and shoots

ADDITIVES FOR A GALLON

Essential   **12 mg. Benerva (Vitamin B1 tablets)**
2 heaped teaspoons tartaric acid

•Advisable 1 nutrient tablet or teaspoonful ammonium
phosphate
½ teaspoon Pectinol, Pectolase

Optional   **½ teaspoonful potassium phosphate**
¼ teaspoonful Epsom salts
½ teaspoonful succinic acid (for 2 year maturing)

OAK LEAF WINE

Ingredients:	*British*	*Metric*	*U.S.A*
Oak leaves	1 gal.	4½ litres	1 gallon
Sugar	2½ lb.	1¼ kg.	2 lb.
White grape concentrate	½ pint	300 mls.	½ pint
Sauternes yeast			
Additives as above			
Water to 1 gallon (4½ litres)			

Make a yeast starter in a wine bottle with a dessertspoonful of grape concentrate (1 U.S.A tablespoon) plus a cup of cold water and the yeast. Plug bottle with cotton wool. When this is fermenting actively collect the oak leaves.

Boil up 4 pints of water (2¼ litres) and pour it over the oak leaves in a plastic bucket. Cover and leave for 24 hours. Strain off the liquid into a gallon jar, add sugar, grape concentrate and additives plus 1 pint of cold water. Stir well and add yeast starter. Ferment at 70°–75°F. (21°–24°C.) until dry (about 3–4 weeks). The jar can be topped up with cold water once fermentation has died down somewhat.

When fermentation is complete, rack into another jar, top up with water and fit a fermentation lock or a bored cork plugged with cotton wool. Mature for 3 months to 2 years.

The wine requires sweetening before drinking at the rate of ½ lb. sugar per gallon (50 gm. per litre).

This wine tends to resemble Sauternes, and if *part* of the sweetening process is done with glycerine (from chemist) this effect is enhanced.

VARIATIONS ON OAK LEAF WINE

The main recipe is for oak leaves gathered in the middle of the summer. It is possible to make a lighter wine by using oak leaves in the spring and also to make a nutty wine using leaves which are browning in autumn. The latter is more suitable as an aperitif.

WALNUT LEAF WINE

Ingredients: 1 gallon of walnut leaves (4½ litres)

Remaining ingredients and method as for Oak Leaf wine. Unlike Oak Leaf, walnut leaves are best gathered only in mid-summer.

VINE PRUNINGS (FOLLY WINE)

Ingredients: 5 lb. vine prunings (2¼ kg. metric, 4 lb. U.S.A.).

Other ingredients and method as for Oak Leaf wine.

BRAMBLE TIP WINE

Ingredients: 1 gallon bramble tips (4½ litres metric, 1 gallon U.S.A.).

Remaining ingredients and method as for Oak Leaf wine.

NETTLE WINE

Ingredients: 2 quarts young nettle tops (2¼ litres metric, 3 pints U.S.A), plus ½ oz. root ginger (14 gm. metric, ½ oz. U.S.A.).

Remaining ingredients as for Oak Leaf wine.

The method differs slightly. The nettle tops are boiled in the water with the ginger for half an hour and the liquid strained over the sugar and other additives—except the yeast and pectic enzyme. The latter two are added when the must is at room temperature.

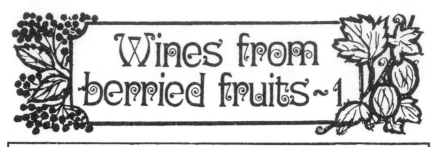

Wines from berried fruits ~ 1

ADDITIVES FOR 1 GALLON

Essential 1 tablet Benerva (3 mg. Vitamin B1 tablet)
2 level teaspoons tartaric acid

Advisable 1 teaspoon ammonium phosphate or 1 nutrient tablet
1 teaspoon Pectinol, Pectolase

Optional ½ teaspoon potassium phosphate
¼ teaspoon Epsom salts (magnesium sulphate)
¼ teaspoon succinic acid (for 2 year maturing)

ELDERBERRY WINE

Ingredients:	British	Metric	U.S.A
Elderberries	4 lb.	2 kg.	3¼ lb.
Sugar	3 lb.	1½ kg.	2½ lb.

Additives as above.
Wine yeast—Madeira, Burgundy, Port
Water to 1 gallon (4½ litres)

Method: First make a yeast starter with a dessertspoonful of grape concentrate or the juice of an orange and a cupful of cold water in a wine bottle. Add yeast and plug bottle with cotton wool. When starter is active, collect elderberries and strig them off into a plastic bucket. Crush with a piece of wood, add 5 pints of water and 1 Campden tablet. Cover and leave for 24 hours. Add remaining ingredients, yeast starter, and ferment for 4 days on pulp. Stir twice a day and keep covered in between. Strain off into gallon jar and fix airlock. Top up with cold water when initial fermentation dies down. Ferment to dryness (about 1 month at 75°F., 24°C.). Rack into another jar and top up with water. Fit a bored cork and plug with cotton wool or an airlock. Mature with rackings each four months for at least 1 year.

When wine is mature, sweeten up with ½ lb. sugar per gallon (50 gm. per litre).

BILBERRY WINE

Ingredients: As for Elderberry wine, using 4 lb. bilberries in place of elderberries. This is a particularly good wine as a dessert wine, and it is worth sweetening it up with grape concentrate (red) in place of some of the sugar.

GOOSEBERRY WINE

Ingredients: 4 lb. gooseberries (2 kg. metric 3¾ lb. U.S.A.).
Other ingredients and additives as for Elderberry wine. However, a white wine yeast should be used—Bordeaux, Hock or Sauternes. Unripe gooseberries can also be made into a good sparkling wine—see relative section.

HAWTHORNBERRY WINE

Ingredients: 5 lb. hawthorn berries (2½ kg. metric—4 lb. U.S.A.).
Other ingredients as for elderberry wine. Method differs in that 3 pints of boiling water are poured over berries and these are then mashed in the water with a block of wood. Two extra pints of water are then added plus remaining ingredients except yeast and pectic enzyme preparation. When must is cool, yeast starter and pectic enzyme are added and fermentation proceeds as for elderberry wine.

ROWANBERRY WINE

Ingredients: 5 lb. rowanberries (2½ kg. metric—4 lb. U.S.A.).
Other ingredients and procedure as for Hawthornberry wine.

SLOE WINE

Ingredients: 2 lb. sloes (1 kg metric— 1½ lb. U.S.A.).
Grape concentrate ½ pint (280 mls. metric—½ pint U.S.A.).
Other ingredients and method as for elderberry wine.

OTHER VARIATIONS

Winemakers in various parts have supplies of local wild fruits described as Cloudberries, Blaeberries, Whortleberries, Cranberries, Blaubeere, etc. All of these make good wine along the lines of the basic elderberry wine recipe. The general quantity of berries used is as for elderberries.

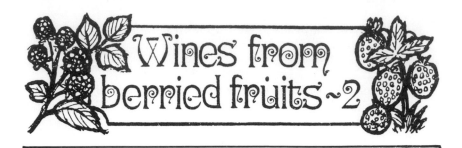

Wines from berried fruits ~2

ADDITIVES FOR 1 GALLON

Essential 1 tablet Benerva (3 mg. Vitamin B1 tablet)
2 level teaspoons tartaric acid
1 level teaspoon grape tannin

Advisable 1 teaspoon ammonium phosphate or 1 nutrient
tablet
1 teaspoon Pectinol, Pectolase

Optional ½ teaspoon potassium phosphate
¼ teaspoon Epsom salts (magnesium sulphate)
¼ teaspoon succinic acid (for 2 year maturing)

BLACKBERRY WINE

Ingredients:	British	Metric	U.S.A
Blackberries	4 lb.	2 kg.	3¼ lb.
Sugar	3 lb.	1½ kg.	2½ lb.

Additives as above
Any wine yeast
Water to 1 gallon (4½ litres)

Method: First make a yeast starter in a clean wine bottle with the juice from a handful of blackberries, 2 teaspoons of sugar and a cupful of cold water. Add yeast and plug bottle with cotton wool.

When actively fermenting, collect blackberries, place them in a plastic bucket and crush. Add remaining ingredients plus 5 pints water. Stir well and add yeast starter. Ferment on blackberries for 3 days and then strain off through muslin or a nylon sieve into a gallon jar and continue fermentation under an air lock. Top up with water as fermentation dies down. When fermentation is complete (about 1 month at 75°F.–24°C.) rack off into another jar and add 1

Campden tablet. Top up with water and fit a bored cork plugged with cotton wool or with an airlock. This wine requires a minimum of 6 months maturing. It can be sweetened up with additional sugar before drinking, at the rate of ¼−½ lb. per gallon (25−50 gm. per litre).

LOGANBERRY WINE

Ingredients and method as for Blackberry wine, replacing blackberries by loganberries at same quantity.

MULBERRY WINE

Ingredients and method as for Blackberry wine, replacing blackberries by mulberries. Mulberries are best collected by placing a sheet under the tree and getting up the tree and shaking it. A particularly fine wine favoured by William the Conqueror, is made by replacing the sugar by its own weight of a mild honey such as clover.

RASPBERRY WINE

Ingredients: 2 lb. raspberries per gallon (1 kg. metric—2 lb. U.S.A.).

Other ingredients and method as for Blackberry wine. In view of the persistent flavour of raspberries, this wine requires at least one year's maturing before it becomes a wine which can be drunk in quantity without cloying.

STRAWBERRY WINE

Ingredients and method as for Blackberry wine, replacing blackberries by strawberries at the same quantity. It is difficult to produce a fine wine from strawberries since the delicate flavour is easily destroyed by oxidation. It become most important to add 1 or 2 Campden tablets to the wine just *before* each racking to avoid this hazard.

MIXED FRUIT

Any of the above fruits can be mixed, and the blend is often superior to the wine made from any single fruit. Care is required with raspberries in that they do not form more than one-third of the 4 lb. per gallon mixture.

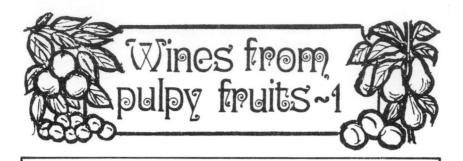

Wines from pulpy fruits ~1

BASIC ADDITIVES FOR 1 GALLON

Essential 1 tablet Benerva (3 mg. Vitamin B1 tablet)
1 level teaspoonful Pectinol, Pectolase

Advisable 1 level teaspoonful ammonium phosphate or 1 nutrient tablet

Optional ½ teaspoon potassium phosphate
¼ teaspoon Epsom salts (magnesium sulphate)
¼ teaspoon succinic acid (for 2 year maturing)

APPLE WINE

Ingredients:	*British*	*Metric*	*U.S.A*
Apples	**8 lb.**	**4 kg.**	**6½ lb.**
White grape concentrate	**½ pint**	**280 mls.**	**½ pint**
Sugar	**2 lb.**	**1 kg.**	**1½ lb.**

Additives as above
Water to one gallon

Method: First make yeast starter using a wine bottle with ¼ pint grape concentrate, ¾ pint water and the yeast. Plug bottle with cotton wool and leave in warm place to ferment (around 75°F, 24°C.). When starter is active, prepare apples by washing them and then either crushing, mincing or slicing and pulping them with a block of wood. Place crushed apples in plastic bucket, add 6 pints water and 1 Campden tablet. After 24 hours add remaining ingredients and additives and the yeast starter. Ferment on the apple pulp for 3 days, then strain off fermenting must into a gallon jar. Top up with water and fit an air-lock.

Ferment to dryness and rack into another jar. Rack again after a fortnight if a heavy sediment appears. In both rackings add 1 Campden tablet.

This wine is generally drinkable after a few weeks, but is at its best after two years maturing. It is normally sweetened slightly before drinking with ¼ lb. sugar per gallon (25 gm. per litre).

APRICOT WINE
Ingredients: 3 lb. apricots (1½ kg. metric—2½ lb. U.S.A.).

Other ingredients and additives as for Apple wine. Method as for Apple wine, except that apricots are first stoned before mashing in plastic bucket. It is important that the straining off process is done efficiently to avoid pulp particles, and a watch must be kept on the wine for a couple of weeks after the first racking in case a pulp sediment builds up, which must be removed by a further racking. Ideally this wine requires one year's maturing with rackings at each 4 months.

PEAR WINE
Ingredients: 4 lb. pears (2 kg. metric—3¼ lb. U.S.A.).

Other ingredients and additives as for Apple wine. Method as for apple wine. If pears are very ripe, add 1 heaped teaspoon tartaric acid.

PEACH WINE
Ingredients: 3 lb. peaches (1½ kg. metric—2½ lb. U.S.A.).
Method and remaining ingredients as for Apricot wine.

CRAB APPLE WINE
Ingredients: 3 lb. crab apples (1½ kg. metric—2½ lb. U.S.A.).
Other ingredients as for Apple wine. Crab apples differ enormously in their acid content, and it may be necessary to add some acid after fermentation to adjust the general balance of the wine. Method as for apple wine.

QUINCE WINE
Ingredients: 6 lb. quinces (3 kg. metric—4¾ lb. U.S.A.).
Remaining ingredients as for Apple wine. Method as for Apricot wine above.

Wines from pulpy fruits ~2

BASIC ADDITIVES FOR 1 GALLON

Essential 1 tablet Benerva (3 mg. Vitamin B1 tablet)
1 teaspoonful Pectinol, Pectolase

Advisable 1 teaspoonful ammonium phosphate or 1 nutrient tablet

Optional ½ teaspoonful potassium phosphate
¼ teaspoonful Epsom salts (magnesium sulphate)
¼ teaspoonful succinic acid

CHERRY WINE

Ingredients:	*British*	*Metric*	*U.S.A*
Cherries	6 lb.	3 kg.	3¾ lb.
Grape concentrate	¼ pint	140 mls.	¼ pint
Sugar	2½ lb.	1¼ kg.	1¾ lb.
Additives as above			
Wine yeast			
Water to one gallon			

Method: Prepare yeast starter in a wine bottle with the grape concentrate, ¾ pint water and the yeast. Plug bottle with cotton wool and stand in a warm place (75°F., 24°C.). When starter is active, wash cherries and place in plastic bucket and crush with a block of wood. Add 6 pints water and 1 Campden tablet. Cover and add remaining ingredients and yeast starter 24 hours later. Ferment on cherries for 4 days, and once a day (with clean hands) extract as many cherry stones from the must as possible. After 4 days strain off must from pulp into a gallon jar, top up with cold water and ferment to dryness under an air-lock.

Add 1 Campden tablet and rack into another jar 3 days later. Rack again after a fortnight if a heavy pulp sediment forms. Otherwise mature for 9 months with rackings each 3 months, topping up the jar with water each time and adding 1 Campden tablet.

This wine can be drunk as a dry wine or be sweetened up before drinking.

DAMSON WINE
Ingredients: **4 lb. damsons (2 kg. metric—3¼ lb. U.S.A.).**
Remaining ingredients and method as for Cherry wine.

RAISIN WINE (Light Table Wine)
Ingredients: **2 lb. raisins (1 kg. metric—1½ lb. U.S.A.). Sugar 1 lb. (½ kg. metric—¾ lb. U.S.A.).**
Remaining ingredients as for Cherry wine, plus 1 heaped teaspoon citric acid. Raisins are best processed by mincing them before pulp fermentation in the plastic bucket. Otherwise method is as for cherry wine.

RAISIN WINE (Dessert Wine)
Ingredients: **3 lb. raisins (1½ kg. metric—2½ lb. U.S.A.). Sugar 2 lb. (1 kg. metric—1½ lb. U.S.A.).**
Remaining ingredients and method as above. The method can be improved by taking 1 lb. of sugar (½ kg. or ¾ lb. U.S.A.) and making it into a syrup by boiling with ½ pint water (280 mls.). When cool this can be stored and be added to the fermenting must once it has absorbed its original sugar. In this way a very high alcohol content can be achieved.

GREENGAGE WINE
Ingredients: **4 lb. greengages (2 kg. metric—3¼ lb. U.S.A.).**
Other ingredients and method as for Cherry wine.

PLUM or BULLACE WINE
Ingredients: **4 lb. plums or bullaces (2 kg. metric—3¼ lb. U.S.A.).**
Other ingredients as for Cherry wine. A slight change in method can be used here by pouring *boiling* water over the plums instead of using sulphite to sterilise them. This assists colour extraction and with the later pulp fermentation will produce quite a deep colour.

43

Citrus wines

BASIC ADDITIVES FOR 1 GALLON

Essential 2 tablets Benerva (3 mg. Vitamin B tablets)

Advisable ¼ teaspoonful tannic acid or grape tannin
1 teaspoonful ammonium phosphate or 1 nutrient tablet
1 teaspoonful Pectinol, Pectolase

Optional ½ teaspoonful potassium phosphate
¼ teaspoonful Epsom salts (magnesium sulphate)
¼ teaspoonful succinic acid

ORANGE WINE

Ingredients:	*British*	*Metric*	*U.S.A*
Sugar	**2 lb.**	**1 kg.**	**1½ lb.**
White grape concentrate	**½ pint**	**280 mls.**	**½ pint**

6 Jaffa oranges or 12 small oranges
Additives as above
White wine yeast—Hock, Bordeaux, Tokay
Water to 1 gallon (4½ litres)

Method: Make a yeast starter with ¼ pint grape concentrate (140 mls.) plus a cupful of cold water in a clean wine bottle. Stir well and add yeast and plug bottle with cotton wool.

When starter is active, wash oranges and thinly peel half of them, taking care not to cut into the white pith, which has a bitter taste. Squeeze juice out of oranges with a juicer, and add it to the peel, sugar, additives and remaining grape concentrate in a plastic bucket. Add 6 pints of water (3¾ litres—5 pints U.S.A.). Stir well and add yeast starter. Cover and ferment at 70°–75°F. (21°–24°C.) for 3 days and then strain off through muslin or a nylon sieve into a gallon jar. Fit an air-lock and ferment to dryness.

Rack into another jar, top up with water and add 1 Campden

tablet (50 p.p.m. sulphite). Mature for at least 6 months, preferably, although it is often drinkable after a few weeks as a *vin ordinaire* and on the other hand will improve for up to 3 years with occasional rackings and sulphiting.

PINEAPPLE WINE

Ingredients: 1 pint canned or fresh pineapple juice (½ litre).

Remaining ingredients as for Orange wine. Method as for Orange wine, except that as no peel is involved, the ingredients can be mixed directly into a gallon jar once the starter is active.

LEMON WINE

Ingredients: ½ pint lemon juice (¼ litre metric and slightly less than ½ pint U.S.A.). This can be bottled or direct from lemons.

Other ingredients as for Orange wine together with method, except that if bottled lemon juice is used the ingredients can be mixed directly in the gallon jar.

LIME WINE

Ingredients: ½ pint lime juice (Roses) (¼ litre metric—½ pint U.S.A.).

Other ingredients and method as for Orange wine except that ingredients can be mixed directly in gallon jar once yeast starter is active.

POMEGRANATE WINE

Ingredients: 8 pomegranates (6 U.S.A.).

Remaining ingredients as for Orange wine.

Method: Having made yeast starter as in Orange wine recipe, peel pomegranates and extract fruit, being careful not to include any of the yellow skin. Crush in a plastic bucket, add remaining ingredients and 6 pints of water (5 pints U.S.A.). Ferment on the pulp for 5 days, then strain off liquor into gallon jar and continue fermentation normally.

GRAPEFRUIT WINE

Ingredients: 1 pint canned or fresh grapefruit juice (½ litre metric—1 pint U.S.A.).

Remaining ingredients as for Orange wine. Method as for Orange wine, except that ingredients can be mixed directly into gallon jar.

Spiced wines

There are a number of traditional country wines, mostly for winter drinking. They are powerful, warming brews and very suitable for heating up for punches and bishops. The following recipes merely make them somewhat easier to make.

CLOVE AND BEETROOT

Ingredients:	British	Metric	U.S.A
Beetroot	3 lb.	1½ kg.	2½ lb.
Sugar	3 lb.	1½ kg.	2½ lb.
Grape concentrate RED	1 pint	½ litre	¾ pint
Vitamin B tablets (3 mg.)	3	3	3
Nutrient tablet	1	1	1
Citric acid	½ oz.	14 gm.	½ oz.
Cloves	4	4	3

Any wine yeast
Water to 1 gallon (4½ litres)
1 teaspoonful Pectic enzyme, added with yeast

Method: First make a yeast starter using ¼ pint (140 mls.) grape concentrate plus 1 cupful of water in a clean wine bottle. Add yeast and plug bottle with cotton wool. Stand in warm place (75°F., 24°C.). When starter is active, scrub beetroots, slice thinly and boil in 5 pints of water (2½ litres metric—4 pints U.S.A.) until tender but not mushy.

Allow to cool and pour over remaining ingredients in a plastic bucket. Add yeast starter and pectic enzyme when at room temperature, and ferment in bucket for 3 days. Strain off through muslin into gallon jar and top up with cold water if necessary. Ferment to dryness under an airlock and then rack into another jar. In actual fact, in view of the sugar content of this must, it is possible that some residual sugar will be left. This is not important since this wine has to be sweetened before drinking in order to achieve balance. Mature in ordinary way for preferably one year.

DANDELION AND GINGER

Ingredients:	*British*	*Metric*	*U.S.A*
Dandelion flowers	2 pints	1 litre	2 pints
Essence of ginger	½ oz.	14 gm.	½ oz.
Grape concentrate	½ pint	280 mls.	½ pint
Tartaric acid	¼ oz.	7 gm.	¼ oz.
Sugar	2½ lb.	1¼ kg.	2 lb.

Plus additives
1 teaspoonful Pectinol, Pectolase
¼ teaspoonful grape tannin or tannic acid
1 tablet Benerva (Vitamin B tablet, 3 mg. size)
Any wine yeast
Water to 1 gallon

Method: Place all the ingredients (except yeast) in a plastic bucket. Add 5 pints of water (2¾ litres metric—4 pints U.S.A.) and add 1 Campden tablet. 24 hours later add yeast and ferment on flowers, etc., for 5 days, stirring twice a day but keeping bucket covered meanwhile. Strain off into gallon jar and ferment out at 75°F. (24°C.). Rack into another jar, top up with water and mature for 6 months. This wine generally requires sweetening before drinking at rate of ½ lb. sugar per gallon (50 gm. per litre).

SPICED ELDERBERRY

Ingredients:	*British*	*Metric*	*U.S.A*
Elderberries	4 lb.	2 kg.	3¼ lb.
Sugar	3 lb.	1½ kg.	2½ lb.
Cloves	¼ oz.	7 gm.	¼ oz.
Root ginger	½ oz.	14 gm.	½ oz.
Grape concentrate	¼ pint	140 mls.	¼ pint

Plus: 1 medium sized lemon
    1 small stick of cinnamon
    1 teaspoonful Pectic enzyme
    1 Benerva tablet (3 mg. Vitamin B tablet)
    1 nutrient tablet or teaspoon ammonium phosphate
    Water to 1 gallon (4½ litres)
    Any good wine yeast

Method: Mash the elderberries in a plastic bucket and pour over them 5 pints (2¼ litres) of boiling water. Cover and leave for 24 hours. Strain off juice into gallon jar, but hold back about 1 pint and bring to boiling pint. Add the bruised ginger, cinnamon, cloves and sliced lemon, and simmer for about 15–20 minutes. Strain the liquor in with the rest of the elderberry juice, add sugar and allow to cool. When cool, add grape concentrate, nutrients, pectic enzyme and yeast. Top up with cold water if necessary.

Allow to ferment to dryness, rack into another jar and top up with water, fit a bored cork plugged with cotton wool.

This wine is generally drunk warmed up on a winter's evening, and normally requires sweetening.

POINTS TO REMEMBER

There are a great many spiced country wines, though they have limited use mainly in winter when served hot. Their big advantage here is that the warming ingredients—ginger, cloves, and so on, have already been mixed in the wine during fermentation, and a delightful hot drink can be prepared in a couple of minutes merely by heating and perhaps adding some sugar or additional orange squash.

From the above three recipes it is easy to concoct your own wines. There are only a couple of points to remember. Firstly, that the best ingredients for these types of wine are fruits on the one hand and vegetables on the other. Secondly, that one normally adds about 1 oz. (28 gm. metric and just a little below an ounce in U.S.A.) of any mixture of the main spices, which are root ginger, cloves, cinnamon, nutmeg and mace. So just find a recipe for the basic wine—say parsnip, and add in your spices boiled in a little of the juice as described in spiced elderberry above. The spices can of course be boiled in water and the liquor extracted added to the main must when cool.

One last point. It is better to use stick cinnamon and root ginger rather than packeted powdered varieties. Powdered spices tend to produce a slight but annoying haze in some wines which is very difficult to remove.

Some notes on herb wines

Wines made with herbs are really ancient country medicine, and their use has been known for thousands of years in all parts of the world. Alcohol is one of the most efficient methods of extracting the value of the herb. It must be remembered, however, that although many of these wines are pleasant to drink as wines, some have astringent flavours, and are included for their original medicinal purpose. Yarrow, for instance, is such a wine. It is recommended for use when one has a cold coming on and to relieve catarrh. I tried it some years ago, and it definitely worked, though I would not like to drink it regularly for pleasure.

In order to prevent confusion, I have given the common name of the herb in Britain plus its Latin name so that it can be identified in other parts of the world. When herbs are out of season, or for townsfolk who might not know what they look like, I have given the alternative of dried packeted herbs as supplied by herbalists. These are standard packs of 2 oz. and one packet is sufficient for 1 gallon of wine.

herb wines ~1

BASIC ADDITIVES FOR 1 GALLON

Advisable 1 tablet Benerva (3 mg. Vitamin B1 tablets)
        1 nutrient tablet or level teaspoon ammonium
          phosphate
        1 teaspoonful Pectic enzyme (Pectinol etc.)

Optional   ¼ teaspoonful Epsom salts (magnesium sulphate)

BALM WINE *(Melissa officinalis)*

Ingredients:	*British*	*Metric*	*U.S.A*
Balm leaves	1 quart	1⅛ litre	2 pints
White grape concentrate	2 pints	1⅛ litre	1¾ pints
Sugar	1 lb.	½ kg.	¾ lb.

Additives as above
Water to 1 gallon (4½ litres)
Any wine yeast
1 packet of dried leaves can replace the fresh

Method: Place all the ingredients in a plastic bucket, top up to 1 gallon (4½ litres) with cold water, stir well to dissolve and add yeast. Cover and ferment for 5 days on the leaves at a temperature of 70°F. (21°C.) approx. Strain off into a gallon jar, fit an air lock and ferment to conclusion. Rack into another jar, top up with water and fit a bored cork plugged with cotton wool. Mature for several months, with an occasional racking and topping up as before. The wine will probably require sweetening before drinking.

Balm wine was used to reduce fevers by inducing perspiration.

BORAGE *(Borage officinalis)*. Used for chest complaints and fevers. Ingredients and method as for Balm wine, except that only 1 pint borage leaves required (½ litre metric—1 pint U.S.A.).

BURDOCK *(Arctium Lappa)*. Used for blood purifying. Ingredients and method as for Balm wine, but quantity of burdock leaves is 1 lb. (½ kg. metric—¾ lb. U.S.A.), or 1 packet of dried leaves.

BURNET *(Sanguisorba officinalis)*. Used as an astringent tonic. Ingredients and method as for Balm wine except that 2 quarts of flowers are required (2¼ litres metric—4 pints U.S.A.).

COLTSFOOT *(Tussilago farfara)*. Used for coughs. Recipe is in Flower wines section.

COMFREY *(Symphytum officinalis)*. Used for chest troubles. Quantity of comfrey roots required are 5 roots per gallon. Remaining ingredients as for Balm wine. The roots are washed, peeled and cut into small pieces and pulp fermented in the ordinary way as with the leaves in Balm wine.

DANDELION *(Taraxacum officinalis)*. Used as a laxative. Recipe in section on Flower wines.

ELDER LEAVES *(Sambucus nigra)*. Used for urinary irregularities. Ingredients and method as for Balm wine.

GOLDEN ROD *(Solidago virgaurea)*. Used as a stimulant to promote perspiration. Quantity of golden rod blossoms required is a large double handful, or one packet of dried. Remaining ingredients and method as for Balm wine.

herb wines ~ 2

BASIC ADDITIVES FOR 1 GALLON

Advisable 1 tablet Benerva (3 mg. Vitamin B tablet)
1 nutrient tablet or teaspoonful amm. phosphate
1 teaspoonful pectic enzyme (Pectinol, etc.)

Optional ¼ teaspoonful Epsom salts (magnesium
sulphate)

PARSLEY WINE

Ingredients:	*British*	*Metric*	*U.S.A*
Parsley heads	1 lb.	½ kg.	¾ lb.
White grape concentrate	2 pints	1⅛ litre	1¾ pints
Sugar	1 lb.	½ kg.	¾ lb.

Additives as above
Any wine yeast
Water to 1 gallon (4½ litres)
1 Packet of dried herbs can replace the fresh parsley

Method: Simmer the parsley (minus the stalks) in 4 pints of water (2¼ litres) for 15 min., and then pour over the sugar in a plastic bucket. Stir well to dissolve and cover. When cool strain into gallon jar with the remainder of the ingredients and add the yeast. Top up with cold water if necessary and ferment under an airlock to dryness. Rack into another jar, top up with cold water and fit a bored cork plugged with cotton wool. Mature for a few months. This wine is normally sweetened before drinking.

NETTLE *(Urtica dioica).* Used for rheumatism. Quantities of young nettle tops required are 2 quarts (2¼ litres metric—4 pints U.S.A.). These measures are for nettle tops lightly pressed down only. Remaining ingredients and method as for Parsley wine.

MISTLETOE *(Viscum album).* Used in the Middle Ages and later in South America as a nerve sedative. I have been unable to find the original recipe, but made some a few years back using 1 packet of Heath and Heather's mistletoe per gallon. Remaining ingredients as for Parsley wine. The same method was used. I was unable to find a hysterical winedrinker to try it on, so we drank it ourselves, and curiously from such an unlikely ingredient the wine was quite pleasant.

MOTHERWORT *(Leonurus cardiacu).* This herb has the same history as mistletoe above. It was in fact used with mistletoe, wood betony and a dreadful smelling herb called valerian to produce a famous brew called "Witches Delight", which was in effect the main tranquilliser of the Middle Ages. I would not recommend this brew in view of the appalling smell of valerian, but motherwort can be brewed on its own, using 1 packet of Heath and Heather's dried herbs per gallon, the remaining ingredients and method being as for Parsley wine.

WOODRUFF *(Asperula odorata).* Used for liver and stomach complaints. Woodruff is found in shady woods, particularly in beech woods, and flowers in May and June in Britain. One gallon of flowers are required per gallon of wine, other ingredients being as for Parsley wine. The method differs slightly from Parsley wine in that it is better to pour boiling water over the flowers, and when cool add the remaining ingredients. Then ferment on the flowers for 4 days, keeping the plastic bucket covered, and merely push the flowers beneath the surface once a day. Then strain off into a gallon jar and continue fermentation normally.

YARROW *(Achillea millefolium).* Used for colds and fevers. Quantities used are 1 gallon (4½ litres) of bruised flowers and leaves, or 1 packet of Heath and Heather dried yarrow. Other ingredients and method as for Parsley wine. This is a bitter wine, but on personal experience I can assert that it does clear catarrh!

BIRCH SAP WINE

This wine is a classic among country wines, of Baltic origin and of tremendous antiquity. Most of the instructions concern the preservation of the health of the Birch tree from which the sap is drawn.

The sap is drawn from a *large* birch tree (sycamore and walnut trees can be similarly tapped) in March or April. A one inch brace and bit is used to drill a hole just beyond the bark—not in the middle of the tree—and a bored cork is fitted with a piece of rubber tubing leading down into a gallon jar. The top of the jar is plugged with cotton wool to exclude insects. Six pints of birch sap can generally be collected in forty-eight hours at this time of the year. At this point a wooden plug must be driven into the tree to prevent the tree bleeding to death. If this is done the tree can be used again in succeeding years.

Ingredients:	*British*	*Metric*	*U.S.A*
Birch sap	**6 pints**	**3¾ litres**	**5 pints**
White grape concentrate	**¼ pint**	**140 mls.**	**¼ pint**
Sugar	**2 lb.**	**1 kg.**	**1¾ lb.**
Vitamin B tablets	**12 mg.**	**12 mg.**	**12 mg.**
Citric acid	**½ oz.**	**14 gm.**	**½ oz.**

½ teaspoonful grape tannin
Water to 1 gallon (4½ litres)
Champagne yeast

Method: Mix all ingredients in a gallon jar and add an active yeast. Ferment to dryness at around 70°F. (21°C.) and rack into another jar. Top up second jar with water and fit a bored cork plugged with cotton wool or an air-lock. This wine needs a few months maturing and will improve up to 2 years. Once mature, it is best drunk as a medium dry wine, and this is achieved by sweetening it with ¼ lb. sugar per gallon (British and U.S.A.)—25 gm. per litre metric.

Notes on honey-based wines

A few words of introduction are needed here, since honey is an animal product, and as such is not so fermentable as vegetable or fruit bases. Nevertheless, wines made from honey are probably the oldest in the world's history, and in fact since bees existed millions of years before mankind, the combination of a beehive knocked into a hollow in a storm plus the rain of the storm, probably produced primitive wines long before anyone was around to drink them.

Honey wines are classified as follows:

Mead. This is a wine made from honey and water only, and may be either dry or sweet.

Melomel. This is a wine made from honey and water plus fruit juice.

Cyser. This is a particular melomel, popular in Britain in King Alfred's time, made from honey, water and apple juice.

Piment or **Pyment.** Although this term covers other drinks, it was originally a drink made by the Greeks and Romans, made from honey and grape juice. It is, of course, another special type of melomel.

Metheglyn. This is of Celtic origin, the Welsh word for medicine, and is compounded of honey, water plus herbs of various sorts.

Hippocras. This is a special type of metheglyn, of Roman origin, made from honey, grape juice plus various herbs.

PREPARATION

There are three main points:

1. The best honeys for winemaking are single-blossom honeys

55

such as Clover, Orange blossom, etc., rather than blended honey.

. The best honeys for winemaking are single-blossomed honeys such as Clover, Orange blossom, etc., rather than blended h o n e y .

2. Honey, although very beneficial to the health, does contain bacteria which could harm a wine must. It is necessary therefore to sterilise the must with sulphite (Campden tablets).

3. Since honey is a poor fermenter, it is necessary to aid it with the full range of nutrients and growth factors, in order to obtain a fermentation which is as fast as normal wines.

Apart from the above, the making of mead and allied drinks is similar to normal winemaking.

Meads

ADDITIVES FOR 1 GALLON			
Essential:	*British*	*Metric*	*U.S.A*
Ammonium phosphate	1 teapsn.	4 gm.	1 teaspn.
Potassium phosphate	½ teaspn.	2 gm.	½ teaspn.
Magnesium sulphate			
(Epsom salts)	¼ teaspn.	1 gm.	¼ teaspn.
Vitamin B1 (Benerva)	15 mg.	15 mg.	12 mg.
Tannic acid	½ teaspn.	2 gm.	½ teaspn.
Tartaric acid	1 heaped teaspn.	7 gm.	1 heaped teaspn.
Malic acid	1½ teaspn.	10 gm.	1½ teaspn.

DRY MEAD

Ingredients:	*British*	*Metric*	*U.S.A*
Honey (Clover)	3 lb.	1½ kg.	2½ lb.

Water to 1 gallon (metric 4½ litres)

Yeast—any good Hock or Moselle yeast such as Steinberg, Berncastler, etc.

Dissolve the honey and additives in about ½ gallon of warm

water (2 litres). Stir well to dissolve and then top up to 1 gallon with cold water, and add 2 Campden tablets (100 p.p.m. sulphite). Fit an air-lock, and after 24 hours add the yeast. Ferment in a temperature of 70°−75°F. (21°−24°C.). Allow wine to ferment to dryness, then rack into another jar and top up with water. Fit a bored cork plugged with cotton wool and mature in a cool place. A second racking should be made after 4 months and thereafter at 6 month intervals. Some meads are fit for drinking after a few months while others require a couple of years to mature.

VERY DRY MEAD

Ingredients:	*British*	*Metric*	*U.S.A*
Orange blossom honey	**2½ lb.**	**1¼ kg.**	**2 lb.**

Water to 1 gallon (4½ litres)
Champagne yeast

Method: As for Dry Mead. However, this can also be made into a sparkling wine, by following the method in the Sparkling Wines section.

MEDIUM SWEET MEAD

Ingredients: As for Dry Mead.

The method differs in that the wine is racked when the gravity drops to 15, and again when it drops to 10 should fermentation restart. After this maturing is carried out in the normal way.

SWEET MEAD

Ingredients: Initially these are as for Dry Mead, but extra honey is required as described in method below. A Madeira yeast is most suitable.

Method: In the early stages, proceed as for Dry Mead, but when the gravity has dropped to 5, add ¼ lb. honey per gallon (about 100 gm.) and stir in well. Repeat this procedure whenever the gravity again drops to 5 until fermentation finally ceases. Then rack and mature as for Dry Mead. Further sweetening with honey or sugar syrup can be done before drinking.

SWEET HEATHER MEAD

Ingredients and additives as for Sweet Mead above, except that heather honey is used. The method is the same also. Heather honey imparts a more distinctive flavour, but generally requires more maturing for it to achieve its best.

QUEEN ELIZABETH'S MEAD

The basic ingredients are as for the favourite mead of Queen Elizabeth I of England (Good Queen Bess), but the additives are twentieth century to permit a good fermentation.

Ingredients:	British	Metric	U.S.A
Heather honey	3 lb.	1½ kg.	2½ lb.
Rosemary	½ oz.	14 gm.	½ oz.
Bay leaves	½ oz.	14 gm.	½ oz.
Thyme	½ oz.	14 gm.	½ oz.
Sweet briar	¼ oz.	7 gm.	¼ oz.
Citric acid	½ oz.	14 gm.	½ oz.
Ammonium phosphate	1 teaspn.	4 gm.	1 teaspn.
Potassium phosphate	½ teaspn.	2 gm.	½ teaspn.
Magnesium sulphate	¼ teaspn.	1 gm.	¼ teaspn.
Vitamin B1 (Benerva)	15 mg.	15 mg.	12 mg.
Tannic acid	½ teaspn.	2 gm.	½ teaspn.

Water to 1 gallon (4½ litres)

Madeira yeast

Method: Dissolve the honey and other ingredients (but not the herbs) in 4 pints of warm water, then top up to 1 gallon with cold water and add 2 Campden tablets (100 p.p.m. sulphite) and add the yeast 24 hours later. Ferment to completion (this may leave the wine dry or with some residual sweetness), and rack into another jar, top up with cold water, and fit a bored cork plugged with cotton wool. Mature for about three months, then suspend the herbs in the wine in a small muslin bag. Taste the wine daily until sufficient flavour has been extracted from the herbs. Then continue to mature the wine, and if persistently hazy fine with normal wine finings. The wine may eventually need to be sweetened to balance the herb flavour.

KING ALFRED'S MEAD ALE

This is the type of honey ale drunk in inns in Britain around the eighth century A.D.

Ingredients:	*British*	*Metric*	*U.S.A*
Clover honey	**1 lb.**	**½ kg.**	**¾ lb.**
Hops	**1 oz.**	**28 gm.**	**¾ oz.**
Citric acid	**¼ oz.**	**7 gm.**	**¼ oz.**
Ammonium phosphate	**1 teaspn.**	**4 gm.**	**1 teaspn.**
Magnesium sulphate			
(Epsom salts)	**¼ teaspn.**	**1 gm.**	**¼ teaspn.**

Water to 1 gallon (4½ litres)
Brewer's yeast

Method: Boil the hops in 4 pints water for ¾ hour. Add the honey and a few of the hops during the last five minutes of boiling. Strain off the hops and leach out the hops with warm water until a gallon of liquid has been achieved. Allow to cool, add the other ingredients and when at room temperature add the yeast. Ferment to completion, skimming the surface for the first few days to remove the scum. When fermentation is complete, allow to settle for a few days, then rack into quart beer bottles, leaving about 1 inch between top of ale and bottom of cork, and prime each bottle with a level teaspoonful of sugar. Screw down corks and store in a warm place for 3 days, then move to a cool place to clear. This can be drunk after a few weeks, or when clear.

Melomels

ADDITIVES FOR 1 GALLON			
Essential	*British*	*Metric*	*U.S.A*
Ammonium phosphate	1 teaspn.	4 gm.	1 teaspn.
Vitamin B1 (Benerva)	15 mg.	15 mg.	12 mg.
Magnesium sulphate	¼ teaspn.	1 gm.	¼ teaspn.
Advisable			
Pectic enzyme	1 teaspn.	1 teaspn.	1 teaspn.
Optional			
Potassium phosphate	½ teaspn.	2 gm.	½ teaspn.
Succinic acid	⅛ oz.	3 gm.	⅛ oz.

GOOSEBERRY MELOMEL

Ingredients:	*British*	*Metric*	*U.S.A*
Honey (original recipe used Acacia Blossom)	2 lb.	1 kg.	1½ lb.
Gooseberries	1 lb.	½ kg.	¾ lb.

Additives as above
Water to 1 gallon (4½ litres)
Burgundy yeast

Method: Dissolve honey in 4 pints of water in a plastic bucket, add gooseberries and remaining additives (except pectic enzyme or yeast). Stir well, add 2 Campden tablets (100 p.p.m. sulphite) and leave for 24 hours. Then add pectic enzyme and yeast and ferment on gooseberries for 3 days. The gooseberries can be crushed by hand or with a wooden spoon each day, but must in any case be stirred beneath surface. Then strain off gooseberries and place fermenting must in a gallon jar. Top up with water and fit an air-lock. When fermentation ceases, rack off into another jar, top up with water, add 1 Campden tablet (50 p.p.m. sulphite) and fit a plugged cork. Mature in a cool place. If there is a lot of pulp, a second racking may be needed after about a week, but otherwise the wine matures very fast and can often be drunk within a few weeks after the end of fermentation. This wine is very light and is normally drunk dry, but can be sweetened up to one's own palate.

BLACK MEAD (BLACKCURRANT MELOMEL)

Ingredients:	British	Metric	U.S.A
Blackcurrants	2 lb.	1 kg.	1½ lb.
Honey	2 lb.	1 kg.	1½ lb.
Red grape concentrate	½ pint	280 mls.	½ pint

Additives as for Gooseberry Melomel

Method: As for Gooseberry Melomel, except that blackcurrants can be crushed when first put in the plastic bucket.

NORFOLK RED MEAD (RED CURRANT MELOMEL)

Ingredients: As for Black Mead above, substituting red currants for blackcurrants at same amount.

Method: As for Black Mead.

LA SEYNE (an old Mediterranean recipe adapted for Britain— basically clover and grape hippocras)

Ingredients:	British	Metric	U.S.A
Fresh clover flowers (if fresh not available use 1–2 oz. dried flowers— 28–56 gm.)	½ gall.	2¼ litres	4 pints
White grape concentrate	1 pint	½ litre	1 pint
Clover honey	2 lb.	1 kg.	1½ lb.

Additives as for Gooseberry Melomel

Any hock or Moselle yeast (Steinberg, Berncastler, Zeltinger, etc.)

Method: As for Gooseberry Melomel, except that whereas gooseberries were strained off after 3 days fermentation, the flowers can be left a further 3 days before straining off.

ORANGE MELOMEL

Ingredients:	British	Metric	U.S.A
Canned orange juice	2 pints	1 litre	2 pints
Heather honey	1 lb.	½ kg.	¾ lb.
Sugar	1 lb.	½ kg.	¾ lb.

Additives and yeast as for Gooseberry Melomel

Method: All the ingredients are put in a gallon jar and the jar topped up with cold water. After stirring well, the yeast is added and fermentation continues under an air-lock to completion. Racking and maturing as for Gooseberry Melomel. After maturing, the wine may be improved by the addition of a pinch of grape tannin. A variation for a lighter, quicker maturing wine can be made by using only half the amount of orange juice, but adding ¼ oz. tartaric acid (7 gm.).

PEACH MELOMEL

Ingredients:	British	Metric	U.S.A
Peaches	3 lb.	1½ kg.	2½ lb.
Acacia blossom honey	2½ lb.	1¼ kg.	2 lb.
Additives as for Gooseberry Melomel			
Graves yeast			

Method: The peaches are first stoned, but thereafter the method is as for Gooseberry Melomel. In view of the high pectin content of peaches, pectic enzyme is now essential rather than advisable.

Pyment ~ Hippocras

ADDITIVES FOR 1 GALLON			
Essential:	British	Metric	U.S.A
Ammonium phosphate	1 teaspn.	4 gm.	1 teaspn.
Vitamin B1 (Benerva)	15 mg.	15 mg.	12 mg.
Magnesium sulphate	¼ teaspn.	1 gm.	¼ teaspn.
Advisable:			
Pectic enzyme	1 teaspn.	1 teaspn.	1 teaspn.

PYMENT

Ingredients:	British	Metric	U.S.A
White grape concentrate	1 pint	½ litre	1 pint
Heather honey	2 lb.	1 kg.	1½ lb.
Citric acid	¼ oz.	7 gm.	¼ oz.
Additives as above			
A small pinch of grape tannin			
Sauternes yeast			
Water to 1 gallon (4½ litres)			

Method: Pour all ingredients into a gallon jar, top up with cold water, stir well to dissolve and add yeast. Ferment to dryness under an air-lock at around 70°F. (21°C.). Rack into another jar, top up with water and fit a bored cork plugged with cotton wool. This wine frequently becomes drinkable a few weeks after the end of fermentation, although it is always advisable to put a bottle away for a year or so to see how fine it becomes in that time.

HIPPOCRAS (1)
Ingredients and method are exactly as for Pyment, except that an additional ingredient, ¼ oz. cinnamon (7 gm.) is added at the start of fermentation.

HIPPOCRAS (2)
Ingredients as for Pyment, but in addition 1 knob of root ginger and the juice and peel (no pith) of 1 small orange are used. The ginger and the orange peel are boiled up in a pint of water for about 20 minutes. The liquid is then strained over the honey, and the remaining ingredients (*except* the pectic enzyme or yeast) are added. The jar is topped up with cold water, stirred well. When at room temperature the yeast and pectic enzyme are added, and fermentation then proceeds as for Pyment.

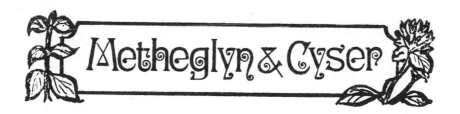

DRY METHEGLYN
Metheglyn is made in the same way as Pyment but it is necessary to use also ONE of the herbs or flowers, either fresh or dried, as set out in detail in the table overleaf.
The equivalent metric and U.S.A. weights for the fresh herbs are:

Metric	2 oz.—56 gm.	4 oz.—112 gm.
U.S.A.	1½ oz.—2 oz.	4 oz.—3 oz.

Ingredients: As for Pyment, but in addition ONE of the following herbs should be used.

	Fresh herbs	*Dried herbs*
Parsley	4 oz.	1 teaspoon
Mint	2 oz.	½ teaspoon
Sage	2 oz.	½ teaspoon
Carroway seeds	2 oz.	½ teaspoon
Meadowsweet	2 oz.	½ teaspoon
Lemon thyme	2 oz.	½ teaspoon
Elderflowers	2 oz.	½ teaspoon
Marjoram	4 oz.	1 teaspoon
Cowslip	4 oz.	1 teaspoon
Balm	2 oz.	½ teaspoon
Mayblossom	4 oz.	1 teaspoon
Mace	1 oz.	¼ teaspoon

A mixture of any of the above herbs can be used as long as the total weight does not exceed the 2 oz.–4 oz. limit above.

Method: The ingredients are assembled as for Pyment and the herbs are also added. This means that for 4 days the fermentation will have to be conducted in a plastic bucket, well covered. The herbs should be stirred beneath the surface once a day. After 4 days, strain off the herbs and continue fermentation as described in Pyment to its conclusion.

SWEET METHEGLYN. As for Dry Metheglyn above, except that the honey is increased by 50%. A small addition of acid—say ¼ oz. (7 gm.)—may be needed before drinking to balance the residual honey.

CYSER. Ingredients and method as for Pyment except that 2 pints of apple juice are added (1⅛ litre metric, 2 pints U.S.A.). The citric adic is omitted. Cyser is the ancient drink of Britain, probably thousands of years old. In its original form it was a straight fermentation of apple juice and honey. If required in this form, the apple juice is doubled and the grape concentrate omitted.

Drinks for a Winter's night

With the exception of the first recipe—Instant Bishop—most of the recipes are around two hundred years old. They arose of necessity when travel was by stagecoach, and hours of bumpy road, in freezing cold and with real danger of death from highwaymen had to be endured until the next coaching inn was reached. On being helped from the stagecoach, the passengers, frozen almost to speechlessness, would be greeted by mine host with a great bowl of punch or bishop, piping hot, which would quickly remove the memory of the past arduous hours. Probably the finest descriptions of these moments occur in Charles Dickens' *Pickwick Papers*.

The recipes given were the best known ones in Britain, but it is a field in which everyone can join to make his own particular mark. Such things as ginger, cloves, mace, cinnamon are interchangeable or can be mixed. Similarly, oranges can be substituted by lemons, limes or grapefruit. Additions of other herbs such as coriander, oregano, marjoram, and so on, can be made. You experiment until you find something better than the original recipe and it is your own creation. You might, if an American, be rediscovering something which George III drank, but what a novel way of celebrating the Boston Tea Party!

BASIC RULES

There are two important points to be remembered.

Temperature. All mulled drinks should be kept hot but not boiling. If they boil, the alcohol starts to boil off. On the other hand, nothing is so dismal as a lukewarm drink of this sort. The ideal temperature is 180°F. (82°C.). In practice this means constant stirring in the saucepan with occasional tastings (in order to add a little of this or that if necessary). When the brew begins to boil round the edge of the saucepan it is ready to serve, and ideally should be served and drunk immediately, putting a metal spoon in each glass to prevent cracking.

Strength. Mulled drinks can be as strong as you wish. If you just want a drink to warm, stick to the recipe. If you want a party to get going quickly, add a few shots of brandy and give each guest a glass as he comes in the door, keeping the brew on a warmer meanwhile. On the other hand, for those not used to the kick of these drinks, it is well to boil up some water separately and to dilute the drinks somewhat with this.

ACTON'S INSTANT LONDON PUNCH

I can make this in three minutes flat. It is a concession to the rush of the twentieth century, but lacks the grace of our past heritage.

Method: Take a glass for each person and fill it two-thirds full with any red wine. Fill *half* the remaining space with orange or lime juice. Pour the lot in a saucepan and heat up. Now add to the saucepan ½ teaspoonful of any of cinnamon, mace, ginger, per person. You can mix them, but not more than ½ teaspoonful total per person. Add 3 cloves per person and also 1 dessertspoonful (an American tablespoonful) of sugar per person. Stir well and when the brew is getting fairly hot, taste it. According to your palate decide if it tastes good, or, if not, whether it needs more sugar (which is probable), more juice (which sometimes happens), or more spice (which is unlikely but possible). Add these little adjustments, stir and retaste. By the time the brew is beginning to boil round the edge you will have arrived at your desired taste. Pour the brew into the glasses, using a metal spoon in each to prevent breakage from the heat. Now add a small shot of brandy, or whisky or whiskey (if you are Irish) and serve around. Drink as fast as you are able. This is not a drink to hover over. It warms you up and makes you feel instant good.

"BISHOP" MATHEWS BISHOP

This is the original recipe of Mathews, the great comedian of the 1830s, the "King" of bishop makers, as described in William Hone's *Year Book* for 1832.

Make incisions in the rind of an orange and stick them with cloves and roast the orange by the fire. Put small but equal quantities of cinnamon, cloves, mace, allspice and a knob of ginger into a

66

saucepan with half a pint of water. Boil it until it be reduced by half. Meanwhile boil a bottle of port wine and, by applying a lighted taper to the pan, burn out a portion of the spirit from it. Add the roasted orange and spice unto the wine and let it stand by the fire for 10 minutes. Rub some knobs of sugar on the rind of an orange and add them to the mixture along with the juice of an orange (not roasted). Grate in nutmeg and sweeten to your taste with honey and you have a Bishop.

LAMBS WOOL (c. A.D. 1730)

It has been said that the British Empire was founded on good English ale, but the following recipe, for four people, *and meant to be drunk immediately,* makes it difficult to comprehend how they ever managed it. You will have to scale it down to your own requirements! Bring in a few friends, but if you insist on drinking your quarter share straight off, start an empire of your own.

Ingredients:	*British*	*Metric*	*U.S.A*
Honey	3 lb.	1½ kg.	2½ lb.
Grated nutmeg	4 teaspns.	4 teaspns.	4 teaspns.
Beer	4 gall.	18 litres	4 gall.
Ginger	2 oz.	50 gm.	1½ oz.

Plus juice of 4 lemons
(Enough for four persons)

Method: Pour all the ingredients into a great pan and heat until the herbs are well blended with the beer. Strain, serve and drink immediately.

TWELFTH NIGHT WASSAIL (eighteenth century)

One sometimes wonders what everyone did before television; well, this is one of the things the English did to end the festivities of Christmas.

Ingredients:	*British*	*Metric*	*U.S.A*
Water	1 pint	½ litre	1 pint
Honey	½ lb.	200 gm.	½ lb. (a bit less)

Plus 3 sticks cinnamon
     2 lemons thinly sliced
     4 cloves
     1 bottle dry red wine

Method: Heat up all the ingredients, stirring well until just below boiling point. Pour into a bowl and float some raisins on top. Add a generous measure of brandy and ignite. The children, armed with spoons now attempt to secure the wine flavoured raisins, and when all have been disposed of, the wassail bowl is distributed among those present and the wassail (good health) toast is drunk.

CAUDLE

This drink dates from the time of Shakespeare. The actual process of caudling was to make the drink as described below and take a quart mug of it, not quite filled, to bed. One got into the chilly bed and carefully brought the quart mug in with one, holding it privily between one's legs so that it warmed the vital parts to a lovely glow. It was then drunk, warming one also inwardly and thus a good night's sleep was ensured.

Ingredients (per person):	British	Metric	U.S.A
Brown ale	2 pints	1 litre	2 pints
Honey	¼ lb.	100 gm.	3 oz.

Plus 1 tablespoon oatmeal (2 tablespoons U.S.A.)
   Pinch of nutmeg
   Juice of a lemon
   1 wineglass of whisky or rum

Method: The ale is poured over the honey and oatmeal and stood by a hot fire or placed in a slow oven until very hot. Strain off the oatmeal and add the nutmeg, lemon juice and whisky or rum. Caudle oneself as above (it's almost worthwhile turning off the central heating).

BOSWELL

This is a modern version of Dr. Johnson's famous "Bishop" which he used to make himself in and around the inns of Covent Garden. The ingredients are the same, only the description has been changed to make it more easily read.

Method: Take a bottle of dry red wine, a sliced orange, 2 table-spoonfuls of honey (4 tablespoons in U.S.A.), 4 cloves and ½ pint of water (about 300 mls.). Put all these into a pan and bring to the boil, but only just. Add a wineglassful of Curacao and one of brandy. Put a spoon in each glass and fill the glasses. Grate a little nutmeg into each glass. Drink immediately.

Some notes on vegetable wines

VEGETABLE WINES

Vegetable wines always present a problem, so some special notes are needed. The main point is that vegetables are very cheap, are in gigantic supply, especially in the country, so why not use the opportunity to make lots and lots of cheap wines?

There is no doubt that very fine wines can be made from vegetables. I tasted one some years ago at the house of Mr. S. W. Andrews, the Chairman of the Guild of Judges, and it was absolutely beautiful. It was, however, *ten years old*. This highlights the problem. The earthiness and rough quality of vegetables requires long maturing to remove.

There are other problems also. Potatoes, for instance, fermented on their own produce significant amounts of certain poisonous alcohols called methyl alcohol and fusel oils. Fortunately we can overcome this problem fairly easily.

The main point is, therefore, that one should not tie up many jars with vegetable wines. Make them by all means, and having initially matured them, put them in any odd containers or bottles which can be stored away in the attic and be forgotten for years on end. Then you can have cheap and lovely wines, but they must be years old.

We are able to speed up the process somewhat by the use of grape concentrate as an additive. The balance is now much better, so maturing proceeds faster, while in the case of potatoes the addition of some grape concentrate pushes the yeast into a more normal path so that the poisonous alcohols are no longer produced in quantity.

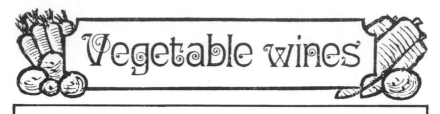

Vegetable wines

ADDITIVES FOR 1 GALLON			
Essential	*British*	*Metric*	*U.S.A*
Vitamin B1 tablets	15 mg.	15 mg.	12 mg.
Malic acid	¼ oz.	7 gm.	¼ oz.
Citric Acid	¼ oz.	7 gm.	¼ oz.
Tartaric acid	¼ oz.	7 gm.	⅛ oz.
Grape tannin or tannic acid	1 teaspn.	1 teaspn.	1 teaspn.
Ammonium phosphate	2 teaspns.	2 teaspns.	2 teaspns.
Advisable			
Pectic enzyme	1 teaspn.	1 teaspn.	1 teaspn.
Succinic acid	¼ oz.	7 gm.	¼ oz.
Optional			
Potassium phosphate	½ teaspn.	3 gm.	½ teaspn.
Magnesium sulphate	¼ teaspn.	1 gm.	¼ teaspn.

Note. With the acids, 1 heaped teaspoon is approximately ¼ oz. or 7 gm. Ignoring the weights, a heaped American teaspoon is the equivalent in each acid for the U.S.A. sized gallon.

POTATO WINE

Ingredients:	*British*	*Metric*	*U.S.A*
Potatoes	5 lb.	2½ kg.	4 lb.
White grape concentrate	½ pint	280 mls.	½ pint
Sugar	3 lb.	1½ kg.	2½ lb.
Any wine yeast			

Method: Old potatoes are best. Scrub them well, cut them into chunks and boil in about 5 pints of water until they are soft but not mashed. Strain the liquid over the sugar and acids. When cool to room temperature add remaining ingredients. Place must in gallon jar and top up with water and add yeast. Ferment in a temperature of around 75°F. (24°C.). When fermentation ceases, rack into another jar, top up with water and fit a bored cork plugged with cotton wool. Thereafter rack each 4 months, topping up with water. At subsequent rackings add 1 Campden tablet. The wine will probably require 18 months maturing, after which it can be sweetened with ¼ – ½ lb. sugar per gallon (7–14 gm.) according to palate, and can be bottled. Further maturing in bottle is required.

BEETROOT WINE

Ingredients and method exactly as for potato wine, using 5 lb. beetroots in place of the potatoes. *Young* beetroots are best in this case to avoid earthiness, and it should be remembered that the wine will lose its deep red colour and become golden during maturing.

CARROT WINE

Ingredients and method as for potato wine, except that only 4 lb. carrots are used per gallon (2 kg. or 3¼ lb. U.S.A.).

LETTUCE WINE

2½ lb. lettuce (1¼ kg. or 2 lb. U.S.A.) are needed per gallon. Other ingredients and main method as for potato wine. The lettuce is boiled for half an hour. Even with the additives, this wine needs about three years before it becomes respectable.

PARSNIP WINE

Ingredients and method as for Potato wine, substituting 5 lb. parsnips (2½ kg. or 4 lb. U.S.A.) for the potatoes. Old country recipes also add 1 oz. root ginger (28 gm. or ¾ oz. U.S.A.) which is boiled up with the parsnips.

PEA POD WINE

Ingredients and method as for Potato wine, substituting 5 lb. peapods (2½ kg. or 4 lb. U.S.A.) for the potatoes. Surprisingly, of all the vegetable wines I have tasted, I have come across more good wines made from peapods than from any other vegetable. It does require a couple of years maturing.

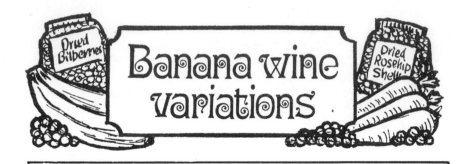

Banana wine variations

ADDITIVES FOR 1 GALLON

Essential	6 mg. Vitamin B1
	1 teaspoonful ammonium phosphate
	½ teaspoonful grape tannin
	1 heaped teaspoonful tartaric acid
	1 teaspoonful pectic enzyme

BANANA AND ELDERBERRY

Ingredients:	British	Metric	U.S.A
Bananas	2 lb.	1 kg.	1½ lb.
Dried elderberries	1 lb.	½ kg.	¾ lb.
Sugar	3 lb.	1½ kg.	2½ lb.

Additives as above
Any wine yeast
Water to 1 gallon (4½ litres)

Method: Slice up the bananas and include the skins. Boil them for half an hour in 4 pints of water and then strain the liquor over the dried elderberries and sugar. Stir well to dissolve, cover and allow to cool overnight. Add the additives and yeast and ferment on the pulp for 5 days. Then strain into a gallon jar, top up with water and fit with an air lock. Ferment to dryness and then rack into another jar. Top up with water, fit a bored cork plugged with cotton wool and mature for about 6 months to 1 year. Sweeten up with half a pound of sugar (about 200 gm.) before drinking, possibly with extra acid also.

During the maturing stage, this wine will at first be very cloudy and mucky. This is due to banana pulp. This is in fact a fairly safe pulp and it will gradually clear downwards leaving a beautifully star

72

bright wine above. Wait until the pulp is down to about 1 inch before racking—approximately 3 months after fermentation ceases.

BANANA AND FIG WINE

Ingredients:	British	Metric	U.S.A
Bananas	2 lb.	1 kg.	1½ lb.
Dried figs	2 lb.	1 kg.	1½ lb.
Sugar	3 lb.	1½ kg.	2½lb.

Additives and yeast as for Banana and Elderberry

Method: As for Banana and Elderberry—the bananas being boiled and the liquor being poured over the chopped figs.

BANANA AND PARSNIP WINE

Ingredients:	British	Metric	U.S.A
Bananas	2 lb.	1 kg.	1½ lb.
Parsnips	4 lb.	2 kg.	3 lb.
Sugar	3 lb.	1½ kg.	2½ lb.

Additives and yeast as for Banana and Elderberry, but add 1 heaped teaspoonful of citric acid in addition to the tartaric acid.

Method: Basically as for Banana and Elderberry, but both chopped parsnips and sliced bananas arc boiled. The water-level may need topping up during the boiling process. When boiling is complete, allow the brew to cool and pour off the liquor away from the pulp directly into a gallon jar. Top up with water and add additives and yeast.

BANANA AND RICE

Ingredients:	British	Metric	U.S.A
Bananas	2 lb.	1 kg.	1½ lb.
Husked paddy rice	3 lb.	1½ kg.	2 lb.
Sugar	3 lb.	1½ kg.	2½ lb.

Additives as for Banana and Elderberry but increase the acid by adding 1 heaped teaspoonful citric acid.

Method: As for Elderberry and Banana. The bananas are boiled and the liquor poured over the husked rice. Fermentation on the pulp for five days then strain off and proceed as basic recipe. This wine needs longer maturing but tends to have a powerful kick having been matured.

BANANA AND PRUNE

Ingredients:	British	Metric	U.S.A
Bananas	2 lb.	1 kg.	1½ lb.
Prunes	2 lb.	1 kg.	1½ lb.
Sugar	3 lb.	1½ kg.	2½ lb.

Additives and yeast as for Banana and Elderberry
Method: As for Banana and Elderberry.

BANANA AND ROSEHIP

Ingredients:	British	Metric	U.S.A
Bananas	2 lb.	1 kg.	1½ lb.
Dried rosehip shells	4 oz.	100 gm.	4 oz.
Sugar	3 lb.	1½ kg.	2½ lb.

Additives and yeast as for Banana and Elderberry, but increase acid with the addition of 1 teaspoonful citric acid
Method: As for Banana and Elderberry.

Cider and Perry

Cider is the fermented juice of apples and perry the fermented juice of pears. They differ from apple wine and pear wine in that while sugar is occasionally added to produce vintage cider or perry, the sugar content of the apples and pears normally carries the fermentation to its conclusion. The resultant flavour is therefore different. Cider is different from apple wine and pear wine from perry. More of the fruit taste comes through in cider and perry than in their respective wines. They are of course lower in alcohol and intended to be drunk by the pint.

Cider is much more common than perry, and is one of the ancient drinks of Britain. Having made it, from the correct blend of apples and in the orthodox manner, it is exactly equivalent, if you are skilful enough in your choice of apples, to the commercial product.

This is something not always realised. Our table wines are attempts, quite often successful, to imitate grape wines. With cider and perry, however, we are on home ground. Our ciders and perrys should be as good as the commercial equivalent. It is necessary to find a model on which to base cider-making. In the West country the model is "Scrumpy", a rough and powerful cider, dry as a bone but possessing tremendous character. Where I live in Buckinghamshire, I wend my way to the Globe Inn on the Grand Union Canal at Linslade, where they serve Bulmers Dry Cider from the wood. This to my mind is cider at its best and is the model to be approached as best we can. We do not have the laboratory advantages of a great cider company, but the basic laws remain the same.

The blending of types of apples is the secret of cider making. The amount of sugar in the apples is of no importance. What is important is the tannin and acid contents. For instance, the common cooking apple Bramley Seedling is very high in acid, too high to eat, but low in tannin. Crab apples, which are easily obtainable, are both high in acid and tannin. Dessert apples are low in both acid and tannin.

The approximate best blend is one-third each of Cooking apples (sharp), Dessert apples (sweet) and Crab apples (bitter sweet). Quite often, however, a medium sharp apple is available—not sweet enough as an eating apple but sweeter than the ordinary cooking apple In this case two parts of these would be blended with one part each of dessert apples and crab apples.

When making perry, only perry pears really make good perry. It is possible to make perry from eating pears, but some addition of grape tannin will be required, or else some of the pear skin must be included in the early stages of fermentation. In addition it is probable that the starting gravity of the juice will be quite high so that the fermentation can be terminated before its normal conclusion to produce a sweet perry.

GENERAL PROCEDURE FOR MAKING PERRY AND CIDER

The fruit is first washed and inspected so that bad or damaged fruit can be discarded or have the bad parts removed.

Next the fruit is chopped into small pieces. In practice this is best done with a potato chipper which speeds the process considerably.

The juice now has to be extracted, and this can be done either with an electric juicer, by means of a jumbo juicer, which is similar to a mincer but with an outlet spout for the juice, or by rough mincing and pressing out in an ordinary press. These presses are obtainable through winemaking suppliers, or can be constructed. Diagram and instructions for construction of one of these are given in a companion book in the Amateur Winemaker series—*Progressive Winemaking.*

As the juice is collected, it should be sulphited with a Campden tablet per gallon of juice (50 p.p.m. sulphite). This is a safeguard against bacterial infection during the collection process.

The starting gravity of the juice should be about 60, and small additions of sugar syrup can be made to achieve this gravity. This syrup is made by boiling up 2 lb. sugar with 1 pint of water (1 kg. sugar with ½ litre water) until the syrup boils clear a few seconds after reaching boiling point. This syrup is allowed to cool to room temperature before use. A quarter of a pint of this syrup per gallon of juice will increase the gravity by approximately 9 points. (Metric this is approximately 32 mls. per litre.) In the U.S.A. a ¼ pint of syrup will increase the gravity by about 11 points with an American sized gallon.

An active yeast starter should have been prepared beforehand, preferably with some of the juices previously expressed, and preferably with a Champagne yeast.

The only additions now required are 2 level teaspoons of ammonium phosphate per gallon (or 2 nutrient tablets), plus one 3 mg. Vitamin B1 tablet per gallon. The yeast starter can then be added and the cider or perry juice fermented under an air-lock.

The finishing gravity now becomes important according to the type of drink being made.

PERRY

The best finishing gravity for perry is about 15, since very dry perry is not as pleasant as medium sweet perry, except for a few people.

DRY CIDER

Here the fermentation should continue to absolute completion.

SWEET CIDER

The cider must should be racked when the gravity has dropped down from 60 to about 45, and a slow fermentation will continue. A further racking when the gravity has dropped to 30 should result in fermentation terminating around 20. At this point 2 Campden tablets per gallon can be added to stun remaining yeast, and the cider finally racked.

MATURING

In all the above cases, the cider or perry is racked off into jars or casks to mature for a couple of months before being bottled. Jars and casks must be kept full during this period.

SPARKLING CIDER

It is essential here to add a teaspoonful of pectic enzyme at the commencement of fermentation, so that the cider will be almost clear by the end of fermentation. The procedure is initially as for Sweet Cider above, but a further racking at gravity 10 is desirable to remove as much yeast as possible, and the cider is bottled when it is at gravity 5. Only good quality cider bottles should be used to prevent any bursting of bottles.

STORAGE

Cider and perry are liable to a darkening in colour if exposed to light or air. Maturing should therefore be in a dark place or in dark jars.

AN ADDITIONAL AID

For about thirty years a company known as Roehm and Hass of Darmstadt, Germany, have been supplying the fruit juice industry with what is known as a pectin-degrading enzyme preparation known as Rohament P. This preparation virtually breaks down the cell walls of a fruit, so that with pressing it is possible to get up to 25% more yield of juice from the fruit. I have tried it myself and it really does work. It is an important substance to use with any pulpy fruit, but in my opinion is at its best in the making of cider and perry.

At long last it is now available in the *Amateur Winemaker*. Instructions for its use are supplied with the packet.

Wines from canned and bottled fruits ~1

ADDITIVES FOR 1 GALLON	
Essential	6 mg. Vitamin B1 tablet 1 level teaspoonful pectic enzyme 2 level teaspoonfuls tartaric acid 1 level teaspoonful ammonium phosphate
Optional	¼ teaspoonful magnesium sulphate ½ teaspoonful potassium phosphate

APPLE WINE

Ingredients:	British	Metric	U.S.A
Canned apple pulp	1 lb. 12 oz.	850 gm.	32 fl. oz.
Sugar	2 lb.	1 kg.	1½ lb.
White grape concentrate	¼ pint	150 mls	¼ pint
Plus Sherry yeast			

Water to 1 gallon (4½ litres)

Method: Empty all ingredients except yeast into a plastic bucket and top up to 1 gallon with cold water. Add 1 Campden tablet and cover. Leave for 24 hours then add yeast. Ferment on pulp for 3 days then strain off into a gallon jar and continue fermentation under an air-lock to completion.

Rack off into another jar and top up with water, fit a bored cork plugged with cotton wool, and mature at around 55°F. (13°C.).

This wine is intended as a dry wine and as such will mature in a matter of a few months. If the initial sugar content is increased by 50% it will contain more alcohol and can be sweetened up and drunk after about eight weeks from the end of fermentation, although will improve with keeping up to 2 years.

APRICOT WINE

Ingredients: One 15 oz. tin apricot pulp (400 gm. metric—15 oz. U.S.A.). Other ingredients as for apple wine.

Method: Exactly as for apple wine.

BILBERRY or WHORTLEBERRY WINE

Ingredients: 1 lb. bottle or can bilberries or whortleberries (½ kg. metric or 15 oz. U.S.A.).

Other ingredients as for Apple wine, except that in addition ½ teaspoonful grape tannin is required.

Method: The bilberries are first crushed in a basin but thereafter the instructions are exactly as for Apple wine.

BLACKBERRY WINE

Ingredients: One 15 oz. tin blackberries (400 gm. metric—15 oz. U.S.A.).

Other ingredients as for Apple wine, except that red grape concentrate is used.

Method: As for Apple wine.

BLACKCURRANT WINE

Ingredients:	British	Metric	U.S.A
Canned blackcurrants	1 lb.	½ kg.	¾ lb.
Red grape concentrate	¼ pint	150 mls.	¼ pint
Sugar	3 lb.	1½ kg.	2½ lb.

Additives as for apple wine, but omitting tartaric acid.

Method: As for Apple wine. This is intended as a sweet wine and should be sweetened with sugar or sugar syrup before drinking.

BLACK CHERRY WINE

Ingredients:

	British	Metric	U.S.A
Canned black cherries	28 oz.	800 gm.	20 oz.
Sugar	3 lb.	1½ kg.	2½ lb.

Additives as for Apple wine
Burgundy or Port yeast
Water to 1 gallon (4½ litres)

Method: As for apple wine. Note, cherries vary enormously in their acid content, so that although there is sufficient acid for the fermentation, a little more—citric—may need to be added before drinking. It will also need sweetening, so that both processes should go on together—a little acid and a little sugar until the flavour is right for you.

Wines from canned and bottled fruits ~ 2

ADDITIVES FOR 1 GALLON

Essential 6 mg. Vitamin B1
1 level teaspoonful pectic enzyme
2 level teaspoonfuls tartaric acid
1 level teaspoonful ammonium phosphate

Optional ¼ teaspoonful magnesium sulphate
½ teaspoonful potassium phosphate

GOOSEBERRY WINE

Ingredients:	British	Metric	U.S.A
Canned gooseberries	1 lb. 4 oz.	600 gm.	1 lb.
Sugar	2½ lb.	1¼ kg.	2 lb.

Additives as above
Sauternes or all purpose yeast
Water to 1 gallon (4½ litres)

Method: Crush the gooseberries in a plastic bucket, add the remaining ingredients and top up with water to 1 gallon. Stir well to dissolve sugar and add 1 Campden tablet (50 p.p.m. sulphite). Add the yeast 24 hours later and ferment on the pulp of the gooseberries for three days. Then strain off and continue fermentation in a gallon jar fitted with an air-lock. When fermentation is complete (about 1 month at 70°F. (21°C.) down to 2 weeks at 80°F. (27°C.)) add 1 Campden tablet and rack into another jar. It will help at this stage if the wine is strained through a nylon sieve or a piece of muslin, to remove pieces of pulp, but not a severe straining which would allow too much air to reach the wine. Top up second jar with water, fit a bored cork plugged with cotton wool and mature in a cool place. This wine tends to mature fast and can be drunk as a *vin ordinaire* after a further 8 weeks, but will obviously benefit from lengthier maturing. It can be slightly sweetened by the addition of ¼ lb. sugar per gallon (112 gm. metric and about 3 oz. sugar per gallon U.S.A.).

GRAPEFRUIT WINE

Ingredients:	British	Metric	U.S.A
Canned grapefruit segments	1 lb. 3 oz.	600 gm.	1 lb.
Sugar	2 lb.	1 kg.	1½ lb.
Grape tannin	1 teaspn.	1 teaspn.	1 teaspn.

Additives as for Gooseberry wine but omit tartaric acid
White wine yeast
Water to 1 gallon (4½ litres)

Method: As for gooseberry wine. This recipe produces a dryish wine with a slight bite similar to an aperitif. Although a heresy, it is very pleasant as a long summer drink mixed with ice and chilled tonic water. Lychee wine can be made in the same way.

LOGANBERRY WINE

Ingredients:	British	Metric	U.S.A
Canned loganberries	1 lb. 14 oz.	1 kg.	1½ lb.
Sugar	3 lb.	1½ kg.	2½ lb.

Additives as for Gooseberry wine
Bordeaux yeast
Water to 1 gallon (4½ litres)

Method: As for Gooseberry wine. When the wine is matured, it should be sweetened with up to ½ lb. sugar per gallon (225 gm. per 4½ litres or 6 oz. per gallon U.S.A.). This may also require perhaps half a teaspoonful of citric acid to balance, depending on taste.

MANDARIN ORANGE WINE

Ingredients and method as for Grapefruit wine above, replacing grapefruit segments by mandarin oranges. When matured can be sweetened up if desired.

PEACH WINE

Ingredients and method as for Gooseberry wine, replacing gooseberries with canned peach slices. It is advisable, however, to double the amount of pectic enzyme.

PINEAPPLE WINE

Ingredients and method as for gooseberry wine, replacing gooseberries with pineapple slices, chunks or rings. This wine matures fast and can be drunk early, especially if chilled.

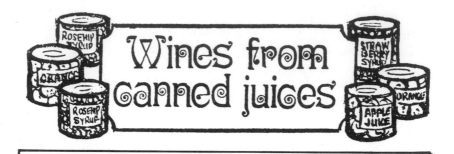

Wines from canned juices

ADDITIVES FOR 1 GALLON

Essential   1 level teaspoonful pectic enzyme
1 level teaspoonful ammonium phosphate

Advisable 6 mg. Vitamin B1

Optional   ¼ teaspoonful magnesium sulphate

Note. All these wines are intended for *vin ordinaires*. They should be made in 5 or 10 gallon lots for everyday drinking, and most of them are drinkable as an honest rough wine within weeks of the end of fermentation.

APPLE WINE

Ingredients:	*British*	*Metric*	*U.S.A*
Canned apple juice	46 fl. oz.	1¼ litres	40 fl. oz.
Sugar	2 lb.	1 kg.	1¾ lb.
Citric acid	½ teaspn.	½ teaspn.	½ teaspn.

Additives as above
White wine yeast
Water to 1 gallon (4½ litres)

Method: Pour all ingredients into a gallon jar and top up with water. Stir well to dissolve sugar and add yeast. Fit an air-lock and place in a warm place around 75°F. (24°C.). When fermentation has almost finished (about 2–3 weeks) add 1 Campden tablet and rack the wine into another jar about 5 days later. Top up with water, fit a bored cork plugged with cotton wool and place in a cool place.

The wine is normally drinkable as soon as it is clear, and this normally only takes a few weeks.

If it is intended to make a sweet wine, the sugar should be increased by 50% and the citric acid doubled. The wine is then finally sweetened just before drinking with ¼ – ½ lb. sugar per gallon according to taste (25–50 gm. per litre).

Note. In the following, the method of preparation is exactly as for Apple wine. In place of apple juice the following should be used, with slight variations in acid or tannin where noted.

	British	*Metric*	*U.S.A*
APRICOT CONCENTRATE	¾ lb.	300 gm.	¾ lb.
BLACKCURRANT (Ribena, etc.)	12 fl. oz.	320 mls.	12 fl. oz.
GRAPEFRUIT JUICE Omit citric acid	1 pint	½ litre	1 pint
ORANGE JUICE Omit citric acid	1 pint	½ litre	1 pint
ROSEHIP SYRUP Increase citric acid to 1 teaspoonful	12 fl. oz.	320 mls.	12 fl. oz.
STRAWBERRY SYRUP Add ½ teaspoonful grape tannin. See note below also.	12 fl. oz.	320 mls.	12 fl. oz.

The general principle in using canned juices is that they are very easy to use, are not in any way messy, which is important in city flats, and since the juices themselves are already sterile, the busy business man can prepare 5 or 10 gallons in a matter of minutes only. The wine must have virtually no problems, and can be left unattended until fermentation has finished, and there are rarely any clearance problems. These wines but seldom find their way to the prizewinners bench, but as a provider of general drinking wine in quantity they are almost unsurpassed.

A special word is required about strawberry wine. The flavour of this wine is so delicate that it is easily lost. Ideally the yeast starter should be prepared in advance with a little of the juice and water. Secondly, fermentation should be conducted at a cooler temperature (65°–70°F., 18°–21°C.) which takes a couple of weeks longer. Campden tablets are absolutely essential at racking times in order to prevent oxidation which can quickly ruin this otherwise very delicate wine.

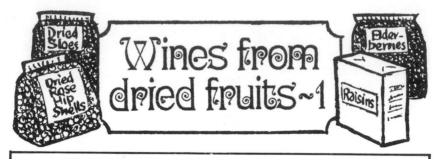

Wines from dried fruits ~1

ELDERBERRY WINE

Ingredients:	British	Metric	U.S.A
Dried elderberries	1 lb.	½ kg.	¾ lb.
Sugar	2 lb.	1 kg.	1 lb.
Grape concentrate, white or red	½ pint	280 mls.	½ pint

Additives as above
Bordeaux or Burgundy yeast
Water to 1 gallon (4½ litres)

Method: Pour about 4 pints (2 litres) of boiling water over the elderberries and sugar in a plastic bucket, stir to dissolve. When down to room temperature add remaining ingredients including yeast. Ferment on the elderberries for 7 days, stirring the must at least once a day and keeping the bucket covered in between. Then strain must into a gallon jar, fit an air-lock and ferment to dryness.

Rack off into another jar, top up with water, add 1 Campden tablet and mature for up to 1 year with racking each 6 months.

The wine can be made into a sweet wine by the introduction of an extra pound (½ kg.) sugar during fermentation, preferably in syrup form. This will provide the extra alcohol required and final sweetening can be done just before drinking. It is probable here that a little extra acid (say 1 teaspoonful per gallon) will be needed and tartaric acid is best for this purpose.

SPECIAL NOTE

Many of the fruits described on this and the opposite page are only obtainable from winemaking suppliers. Due to fluctuating supplies slightly mouldy berries are occasionally obtained. The mould cannot normally be seen but it can be smelled—a dank sort of smell which will carry through to the wine. Avoid these berries. Fortunately, with the increase in winemaking the turnover of fruit is becoming faster and this trouble less frequent.

BILBERRY WINE

Ingredients and method as for Elderberry wine opposite, substituting dried bilberries for the dried elderberries.

BANANA WINE

Ingredients:	British	Metric	U.S.A
Dried bananas	12 oz.	350 gm.	10 oz.
Sugar	2 lb.	1 kg.	1½ lb.
White grape concentrate	½ pint	300 mls.	½ pint

Additives and yeast as for elderberry wine

Method: Simmer the bananas in 3 pints of water (1½ litres for half an hour and pour the liquor over the sugar. When down to room temperature add the remaining ingredients and continue as for Elderberry wine, except that fermentation can commence in jar when cool.

SULTANA OR WHITE RAISIN WINE

Ingredients:	British	Metric	U.S.A
Sultanas (white raisins)	1 lb.	½ kg.	¾ lb.
Bananas (fresh ones)	2 lb.	1 kg.	1½ lb.
Sugar	2 lb.	1 kg.	1½ lb.

Additives as for Elderberry wine, but increase the citric acid to 2 teaspoonfuls

Method: Boil the bananas without the skins for half an hour and strain the liquor over the sultanas and sugar. When cool add the remaining additives and continue as for Elderberry wine, except that the sultanas are strained off after 4 days only.

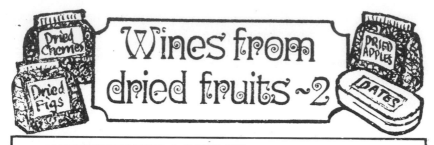

Wines from dried fruits ~2

ADDITIVES FOR 1 GALLON	
Essential	2 teaspoonfuls citric acid
	1 teaspoonful ammonium phosphate
	15 mg. Vitamin B1
	2 teaspoonfuls pectic enzyme
Optional	½ teaspoonful potassium phosphate
	¼ teaspoonful magnesium sulphate

APRICOT WINE

Ingredients:	British	Metric	U.S.A
Dried apricots	1 lb.	½ kg.	¾ lb.
Sugar	2½ lb.	1¼ kg.	2 lb.

Additives as above
White wine yeast
Water to 1 gallon (4½ litres)

Method: Pour about 4 pints (2 litres) of boiling water over the apricots and sugar in a plastic bucket. Stir to dissolve. When down to room temperature, and not before, add the remaining additives and yeast. Ferment on the pulp for 4 days stirring the pulp beneath the surface twice daily.

Strain off into a gallon jar, top up with water and fit an air-lock. Ferment at around 70°F. (21°C.) until complete. Rack into another jar, top up with water, add 1 crushed Campden tablet and fit a bored cork plugged with cotton wool.

Observe the jar after about 10 days, and if a heavy pulp sediment has formed, rack once more with topping up and a Campden tablet. Otherwise mature in a cool place and rack the wine after six months. It will probably be drinkable at this time but will improve for at least another year.

This is normally a medium sweet wine, but can be drunk drier or sweeter according to taste.

APPLE WINE

Ingredients:	*British*	*Metric*	*U.S.A*
Dried apples	2 lb.	1 kg.	1½ lb.
Sugar	2 lb.	1 kg.	1½ lb.

Additives and yeast as for Apricot wine, but replace citric acid
by tartaric acid.

Method: As for Apricot wine.

CHERRY WINE

Ingredients:	*British*	*Metric*	*U.S.A*
Dried cherries	1 lb.	½ kg.	1 lb.
White grape concentrate	½ pint	300 mls.	½ pint
Sugar	1½ lb.	¾ kg.	1½ lb.

Additives and yeast as for Apricot wine, but omit citric acid.

Method: As for Apricot wine, but add grape concentrate when
cool.

DATE WINE

Ingredients:	*British*	*Metric*	*U.S.A*
Dates	2 lb.	1 kg.	1½ lb.
White grape concentrate	½ pint	300 mls.	½ pint
Sugar	1 lb.	½ kg.	1 lb.

Additives and yeast as for Apricot wine, but reduce citric acid
to 1 teaspoonful.

Method: As for Apricot wine, but add grape concentrate when
cool.

FIG WINE

Ingredients:	*British*	*Metric*	*U.S.A*
Dried figs	2 lb.	1 kg.	1½ lb.
Sugar	1½ lb.	¾ kg.	1¼ lb.

Additives as for Apricot wine, but in addition add 1 teaspoonful grape tannin.

Method: As for Apricot wine.

PEACH WINE

Ingredients and method as for Apricot wine, replacing dried
apricots with dried peaches.

PRUNE WINE

Ingredients:	British	Metric	U.S.A
Prunes	4 lb.	2 kg.	3 lb.
Sugar	2 lb.	1 kg.	1½ lb.

Additives as for Apricot wine, but in addition add 1 teaspoonful grape tannin.

Method: As for Apricot wine.

Rhubarb wine

Rhubarb wine requires a special chapter on its own because it has special problems. This is rather unfortunate, because it is one of the first wines which beginners tend to make. You come across a book such as this, take it home and, on reading it, become enthused with the idea of great quantities of drink at fabulously low cost, and you want to get weaving straight away. In the garden are great luscious stalks of Champagne rhubarb, so why not start with that? It sounds good, and undoubtedly rhubarb does make a very fine wine, but it does have problems.

The problems arise from two causes. Firstly, rhubarb contains a poisonous acid called oxalic acid and secondly, for reasons partly unknown, it sometimes causes destruction of the yeast which floats around in clumps in the wine in a most disgusting fashion. This causes beginners to view winemaking as an advanced science whereas it is really comparatively easy.

The two problems are resolved by first treating the rhubarb in a different fashion from that advocated in old country winemaking books, and, secondly, by ensuring the conditions ideal for the yeast.

Now, the main acid in rhubarb is malic acid, a good fermenting acid and valuable in maturing. It is present in almost every cell of the plant. The poisonous acid (oxalic acid) is in little lumps called nodules which are scattered here and there in the plant. If the juice is extracted with boiling water as was the normal way, then the oxalic acid is dissolved into the liquor along with the flavour and the helpful malic acid. At this point chalk was added to get rid of all the acids and then citric acid was added to allow fermentation to proceed. This was a very hit-and-miss method which frequently allowed fermentations to proceed without sufficient acid. The result was an evil smelling concoction. It is this obsession with oxalic acid which is at the root of the problem. People quite often eat large amounts of stewed rhubarb without ill results. I have never heard of anyone dying of oxalic poisoning from rhubarb. The *Financial Times*, in an article on pollution recorded deaths from eating an excess of strawberries which also contain oxalic acid, and since spinach also contains fair quantities of this acid, spinach addicts might expect a similar fate. The reason that rhubarb, strawberries and spinach do not pose potential hazards is that they are not normally eaten in excess.

With rhubarb we can, in fact, improve the situation. It is a question of extracting the juice without extracting too much oxalic acid. Then the normal acid of the fruit—malic acid—can do its job quite naturally. This is done either by getting the juice in a liquidiser or a fruit juice mincer, or by using cold extraction processes. The nodules of oxalic acid mainly get by-passed.

The second problem of yeast destruction may well be caused by the first. Old recipes for rhubarb wine advocate the addition of chalk to remove the acid. Very rarely do they say how much, or if they do it is based on an average season. As a result the must is sometimes alkaline rather than acid. A yeast likes an acid must and does not function properly otherwise. It is a living organism and the winemaker must never forget this fact.

Here, then, is how to make rhubarb wine the simple way. I must admit that I put in the optional additives just to be sure, but it works fairly quickly without them.

OPTIONAL ADDITIVES

Vitamin B tablets	6 mg.		
Grape tannin	½ teaspoonful		
Ammonium phosphate	1 teaspoonful		
Pectic enzyme	1 teaspoonful		
Ingredients:	*British*	*Metric*	*U.S.A.*
Rhubarb	4 lb.	2 kg.	3 lb.
Sugar	2 lb.	1 kg.	1½ lb.
Champagne yeast			
Water to make 1 gallon (4½ litres)			

Method: First make a yeast starter by taking a clean wine bottle and filling it with one part fruit juice and 3 parts water. Any fruit juice will suffice for this (a large orange, canned juice, etc.). Add 1 dessertspoonful of sugar (an American tablespoonful), mix well to dissolve sugar, add yeast and plug the bottle with cotton wool. Place in a warm temperature around 75°F. (24°C.). After about 24 hours it should be fermenting. Then pull the rhubarb, wash it and cut it into 2 inch chunks and slice each chunk into three. Place rhubarb in a plastic bucket. Add sugar and top up to 1 gallon with water (cold) and add yeast starter. If the optional additives are used, add them at this point.

Ferment the fruit for 7 days, then strain off into a gallon jar and continue fermentation to its completion. Rack off into a second jar, top up with water and fit a bored cork plugged with cotton wool. Mature for about 6 months. At this point you will have a dry table wine, which should be bottled and bottles stood upright. The corks can alternatively be tied down. The reason for this is that frequently this wine will undergo what is known as a malo-lactic fermentation which results in gas being generated in the bottle, so that a sparkling wine results.

If you have a liquidiser or similar apparatus, then the juice should be expressed from the rhubarb straight into the gallon jar, the jar topped up and the yeast starter added.

The wine can, of course, be made into sweet wine by feeding the must with an extra pound of sugar (½ kg.) gradually to increase the alcohol.

GRAPEFRUIT APERITIF

Ingredients:	British	Metric	U.S.A
Grapefruit (small)	9	9	9
Sultanas	½ lb.	250 gm.	½ lb.
Raisins	¼ lb.	100 gm.	¼ lb.
Sugar	2½ lb.	1 kilo	2 lb.

Plus 1 teaspoon ammonium phosphate or nutrient tablet
1 teaspoon liquid pectic enzyme
1 teaspoon Bentonite (Optional)
2 gm. sodium metabisulphite or 2 Campden tablets
General purpose wine yeast
Water to 1 gallon (4½ litres)

Make the yeast starter by heating the juice of 1 grapefruit to boiling point with about 6 fl. oz. (200 mls.) of water and 1 dessertspoon sugar. Pour into a sterilised bottle, plug with cotton wool and leave to cool. When cool, add yeast and a little nutrient. Leave in a warm place (70°−75°F. (21°−24°C.)) and shake the bottle now and then until fermentation commences, which should be within about 24 hours. Cut the rest of the grapefruit in half and express juice on a squeezer. Add 1½ gm. sodium metabisulphite or 1½ Campden tablets. Wash dried fruit thoroughly and mince. Add dried fruit to grapefruit juice with the pectic enzyme, nutrient and water to make up to approximately ¾ gallon (4 litres). Cover and leave 24 hours. Add working yeast starter and ferment on pulp for 3 days, stirring night and morning, otherwise keeping well covered. Strain into a gallon jar and add 1½ lb. (700 gm.) granulated sugar to give a specific gravity of 1080. Top up jar with water to three-quarters full. Fit air-lock and agitate bottle night and morning until vigorous ferment dies down. Add further 1 lb. (450 gm.) granulated sugar (or enough to give a total starting gravity of 1110). Top up jar with water to neck. Fit air-lock and leave to ferment to dryness. Rack into clean jar. Mix 1 teaspoon Bentonite with a little of the wine and blend or whisk with a hand beater. Add to the rest of the wine, stir well and leave to settle out in the refrigerator if possible. After about a week, rack into a fresh jar and top up if necessary with water or another similar sound wine. Add ½ gm. sodium metabisulphite (enough to cover a new penny) or half a Campden tablet, leave to mature for 1 or 2 years, racking once or twice more as necessary. This wine can also be sweetened with ¼ or ½ lb. sugar per gallon once it has matured (25−50 gm. per litre).

ORANGE APERITIF

This is made with Seville oranges obtainable in the third week in January. You must be prepared to expect that this wine will appear completely undrinkable during the maturing period owing to its bitterness.

Ingredients:	British	Metric	U.S.A
Seville Oranges	6	6	5
White grape concentrate	½ pint	½ pint	½ pint
Sugar	3 lb.	1½ kilos	3 lb.

Plus Nutrient tablet or 1 teaspoonful ammonium phosphate
      One 3 mg. Vitamin B1 tablet (Benerva)
      Wine yeast
Water to 1 gallon (4½ litres)

Method: Wash the oranges and peel 3 of them, taking care not to include the white pith. Boil up the peel in 1 pint of water and allow to stand for 24 hours to extract the zest. Extract the juice of the oranges and add it to the sugar, grape concentrate and nutrient in a gallon jar. Top up with water to the shoulder, stir to dissolve, add zest of orange peel and starter. Ferment to dryness, rack and mature. The wine will benefit by being racked from one jar to another every 3 months. It can be bottled after about 1 year, but may not assume its true aperitif flavour under 18 months. Ultimately it can be presented as a dry or sweet aperitif, the latter being made by adding ¼ lb. of sugar per gallon, or even as much as ½ lb. per gallon.

HERBAL APERITIF

One of the commonest methods of making an aperitif in the commercial wine world, is to first make a grape wine and then steep various herbal mixtures in it until sufficient flavour has been extracted from the herbs. This is the purpose of this recipe. It allows you complete scope to develop an aperitif of your own, and the suggested herbal additions given after the recipe are merely a guide for your early experiments.

BASIC WINE

Ingredients:	British	Metric	U.S.A
Red or white grape concentrate	2 pints	1⅛ litre	2 pints

Plus Sugar as required
      Vitamin B1 15 mg.
      Ammonium phosphate, 1 teaspoonful
      Burgundy or Bordeaux yeast
      Water to 1 gallon (4½ litres)

Method: Empty the grape concentrate into a gallon jar, add the nutrients, top up jar to about the 6 pint level (3¾ litres or 5 pints U.S.A.) and add the yeast. Ferment in a warm temperature, 75°–80°F. (24°–27°C.). Meanwhile make up a sugar syrup solution by boiling 2 lb. sugar with 1 pint of water until it boils clear (1 kg. sugar with ½ litre water). Store this for use in a bottle. This syrup is used to increase the alcohol potential whenever the yeast has used up the sugar in the grape concentrate. Ideally this is done with a hydrometer, additions being made whenever the gravity falls to zero, but it can be done by tasting the fermenting wine every few days, and making the additions whenever the wine no longer tastes sweet. Additions are made at the rate of ¼ pint of syrup each time (140 mls. metric—¼ pint U.S.A.). By this method a very powerful wine can be made which obviates any later fortification (most commercial aperitifs are fortified).

When the yeast can take no more sugar (about 6–8 weeks) rack the wine into another jar, top up with water or wine if necessary, fit a bored cork plugged with cotton wool and mature in a cool place.

The wine matures and clears fairly rapidly, so that about 8 weeks after the end of fermentation is the time to add the herbal mixture to give the wine its aperitif character. The herbs are tied in a small muslin or nylon bag and inserted in the wine. This is best done by inserting a piece of glass tubing through the bored cork and tying the herbal sachet near the bottom of the tube. The top of the glass tube is stuffed with cotton wool. By this means the herbal sachet is well down inside the jar. Each day it is swirled up and down a few times to distribute the flavour. The time factor for this process of herb extraction depends on the herbs used and your palate. You therefore have to taste the wine each time until sufficient extraction has been obtained. Then the sachet is extracted from the wine and normal maturing continues. The final decision as to whether the aperitif is to be dry or sweet again depends on personal preference. If, however, you find that by accident you have extracted too much flavour from the herbs, sweetening the wine will help the imbalance to disappear.

HERBAL MIXTURES TO USE

First and foremost I must recommend the vermouth type mixtures sold by prominent winemaking suppliers such as Grey Owl Laboratories, Fermenta, Semplex, etc. In some cases these are almost a perfect match of the herbs used in certain well known commercial aperitifs. I have tried several of these and under the conditions in which I use them find them equal to the commercial equivalent which is about eight times the price in Britain. This use is either with gin, ice and a sliver of lemon as an aperitif or with soda water, ice and lemon as a long summer drink.

Apart from the above, the following can be used either singly or in mixtures. About a couple of heaped teaspoonfuls of the dried herb in the muslin sachet is normally sufficient. Fresh herbs can be used without the muslin bag merely by tying them to the glass tube. Amounts differ here and they are merely used and replaced if necessary by more fresh herbs until sufficient flavour has been obtained.

Parsley
Mint (this would be used if white grape concentrate were used for the basic wine)
Carroway seeds
Lemon Thyme (for a white wine as for Mint)
Marjoram
Mace
Wormwood
Tarragon

Mixtures are best dealt with singly. Thus, for instance, a nice sweet aperitif can be made from a basic white wine which is flavoured up with Carroway seeds. This produces a Kummel type flavour. On top of this is next added a mint flavour until the mint balances the carroway. The final wine is then sweetened and is a quite unusual aperitif, very attractive if lightly chilled. I believe the originator of this unusual combination was "Doc" Harrison of the Wembley guild.

SPARKLING WINES

There are two main types of sparkling wine, that made by the Champagne process and that made by pumping carbon dioxide into a still wine. Let us first dispose of the instant sparkling wine. It is not a patch on the true stuff, but is interesting. You need a soda water siphon into which a Sparklet bulb is inserted. The siphon is filled with a light white or rosé wine and then the top screwed on and the Sparklet bulb fired into it. The siphon is then shaken constantly for about a quarter of an hour. After this the siphon is turned upside down so that the end of the siphon tube projects above the liquid. Then with a napkin held over the spout to avoid undue splashing, the lever of the siphon is depressed, so that the excess gas is expelled. When all is quiet once more, the siphon is uprighted and the head is unscrewed. The wine is then poured into glasses as from a bottle, by first removing the plastic sleeve. Remember to replace the plastic sleeve before refilling.

TRUE SPARKLING WINES

The basis of this is that a light table wine is made and racked into strong champagne bottles. Each bottle is primed with a little sugar so that the secondary fermentation occurs inside the bottle, the corks of which have been tied down or secured with twine. The bottles are inverted and shaken to allow the yeast sediment to fall on to the corks. The necks of the bottles are then frozen and the corks released so that the cork and its frozen ice pellet with the yeast is expelled. The bottle is then topped up with syrup or brandy and resealed and allowed to mature.

You will see from this brief description that a fair amount of time and care is required to make this type of wine. It does have certain hazards also in that any error on your part in overdosing, or in using a badly scratched bottle (which weakens it) may result in a burst bottle. When I made my first sparkling wines, I had young children around the house, so I took the greatest of care, and have never had a burst bottle—I do the same with beer-making. I use champagne bottles that have only been used once, and I use a Clinitest outfit to measure the amount of sugar in the fermented wine. This latter is probably known under other names in various parts of the world, and is used by diabetics to test the sugar content of their urine. If I describe its use you will recognise it under your local name.

CLINITEST

The outfit consists of a small test-tube, a dropper, some tablets and a colour chart. Five drops of wine are put in the test-tube and the dropper rinsed out. Then 10 drops of water are added and following this one of the tablets. The mixture will foam and change colour to either brown, light green, dark green or blue. Blue indicates that there is no sugar left in the wine, dark green indicates there is only 0.25% (a quarter of 1 per cent) sugar remaining. Light green indicates approximately 0.5% remaining. The brown colour reveals that there is *at least* 2% remaining, but does not indicate exactly how much.

This diabetic sugar check outfit only measures invert sugar and would not record any recent additions of sugar to the must, but since these are not required by the recipe, one can be sure that the original sugar will have become invert sugar by the time racking is required.

The first recipe describes in detail the whole process. Once you have the process you can in fact make a sparkling wine out of any light table wine, flower wine or, in fact, from any wine which is about 2 lb. sugar per gallon (1 kg. to 4½ litres) including sugar in the fruit. Red wines, however, are not normally suitable for turning into sparkling wines.

SPARKLING GOOSEBERRY

Ingredients:	British	Metric	U.S.A
Green gooseberries	6 lb.	3 kg.	5 lb.
White grape concentrate	1 pint	½ litre	1 pint
Sugar	1 lb.	½ kg.	¾ lb.

Plus One 3 mg. Vitamin B1 tablet
1 level teaspoon pectic enzyme
1 level teaspoon ammonium phosphate or a nutrient tablet
Champagne yeast
Water to 1 gallon (4½ litres)

Method: Top and tail the gooseberries, add the sugar and pour 4 pints (2¼ litres) of boiling water over them. When cool, crush the gooseberries, add the pectic enzyme, Vitamin B1, ammonium phosphate and the yeast. Ferment on the pulp for 4 days, then strain off into a gallon jar and top up with water. Ferment under an airlock at around 70°F. (21°C.).

When the gravity falls to around zero, start testing with the Clinitest outfit until a dark-green or blue reading is obtained.

Now prepare a special syrup by boiling 1 lb. of sugar with 1½ pints of water (this produces gravity 150 syrup, half the strength of that normally used by winemakers).

Wash out and sterilise the champagne bottles.

Rack the wine from its yeast into a second jar and add the following dosage of 150 syrup according to the reading obtained.

Ingredients:	British	Metric	U.S.A
Clinitest blue, nil sugar	5 fl. oz. per gal.	140 mls. per 4½ l.	4 fl. oz. per gal.
Clinitest dark green	3 fl. oz. per gal.	85 mls. per 4½ l.	2½ fl. oz. per gal.

This will produce a pressure of about 3½ atmospheres or 50 lb. per square inch which is about half that of commercial practice and will assist later processes.

After mixing the sugar in well, transfer the wine to the champagne bottles, leaving a space of about 1½ inches between wine and cork and secure corks with wire. Corks and wires are now easily obtainable from winemaking suppliers.

The bottles should now be stored horizontally at about 50°F. (10°C.) for about 9 months.

The next stage is disgorgement, and the bottles are inverted and shaken to dislodge the yeast sediment so that it settles on the cork. It is a skilled process in the Champagne industry, but most amateurs seem to manage it quite well. It does, however, take a few days of twisting and shaking, once or twice a day, at the end of which all your bottles are upside down.

Now prepare the final dosage, a good one of which is equal parts of brandy and the 150 gravity syrup. Only about half a pint of this mixture is needed for half a dozen bottles.

The bottles are first stood upside down in a bucket of ice to reduce their internal temperature and pressure. Then the necks of the bottles are placed in a freezing mixture such as ice and salt or dry ice. A plug of ice quickly forms in the bottle neck and encases the yeast deposit. The bottle is then held upside down in one hand while the wire is removed with the other. The cork is edged out and directly it discharges itself the bottle is returned to an upright position with one's thumb over the top to prevent undue loss of wine. A dosage of the brandy-sugar mixture is then added and the bottle recorked and wired. The bottles are then stored horizontally for a further period of maturing.

The second sparkling wine has a story. It is the brain-child of Gerry Whitehouse of Torquay, one of the country's leading amateur wine judges, and he entered it in the Judges and Stewards class at the National at Caister in 1970. It was just fractionally better than its nearest rival, but it did not get a prize. I was the judge of this class. It happened quite by accident that, in bottling, Gerry ran out of champagne corks and had to use a few ordinary corks. Under the pressure and the wiring, an ordinary cork spreads out just like a champagne cork, and Gerry grabbed this bottle instead of one of the many correctly bottled ones he had. The rules of the National are strictly observed and I had to disqualify this bottle. At the time, of course, I did not know whose wine it was. There was just this beautiful bottle of wine and myself chatting to each other. I was abjectly apologising to it for what had to occur, and it was balefully staring back at me with an expression which implied "May the Powers of darkness rot your taste-buds." Having finished the judging, I did this wine the honour of drinking a couple of glasses of it (champagne does not keep, once opened). It really was a magnificent wine. As Gerry manages the Rock Walk Hotel in Torquay, I have called it after that establishment.

ROCK WALK CHAMPAGNE (For 5 gallons)

Ingredients:	British	Metric	U.S.A
Apple juice	2½ gal.	11 litres	2½ gal.
Hidalgo white grape con.	½ gal.	2¼ litres	½ gal.
Sugar	5 lb.	2½ kg.	4 lb.

Water to 5 gallons (22½ litres)

Note. In the original, mixed cider apples were used to produce the juice. If these are not available, a mixture of crab apples, cooking and dessert can be used, roughly in equal parts.

Method: Mix the ingredients together and make up to 5 gallons with water. Adjust the acidity of the must to 3½−4 parts per thousand in terms of sulphuric acid. (In the U.S.A. this is 5.3−6.1 parts per thousand in terms of tartaric acid.) Sterilise the must with 1 Campden tablet per gallon (50 p.p.m. sulphite). After 24 hours test gravity and add the yeast starter, using a good Champagne yeast (Gerry uses Respora Champagne or C.W.E. Champagne). Ferment under an air-lock at around 70°F. (21°C.) and when gravity has fallen to 10, add, if necessary, sufficient extra sugar to produce a wine of 10½−11½% alcohol by volume when the wine is dry.

When fermentation ceases, rack into jars and fit bored corks plugged with cotton wool and mature for about 6 months. Pour into champagne bottles and add to each bottle 3 lumps of cube sugar, bottle with champagne stoppers. Store bottles on their sides for a further 6 months to condition.

This alternative method of making sparkling wines does not require disgorgement, since there is so little sediment that it is not worth bothering about.

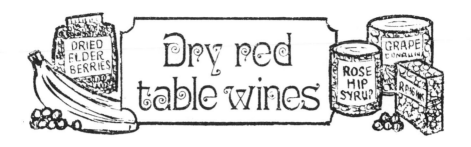

Dry red table wines

DRY RED TABLE WINE (Burgundy type)

Ingredients:	British	Metric	U.S.A
Dried elderberries	½ lb.	¼ kg.	½ lb.
Rose-hip syrup	12 fl. oz.	400 mls.	12 fl. oz.
Sugar	2 lb.	1 kg.	1½ lb.
Tartaric acid	1 teaspn.	1 teaspn.	1 teaspn.
Nutrient tablet	1	1	1
Pectic enzyme	1 teaspn.	1 teaspn.	1 teaspn.

Plus Juice of 1 large Jaffa orange
Burgundy or Bordeaux yeast
Water to 1 gallon (4½ litres)

Method: First make yeast starter by washing out a wine bottle and putting it in the juice of the orange, and 1 level dessertspoonful of sugar, and topping up to the shoulder with water. Shake to dissolve sugar and then add yeast culture and plug bottle with cotton wool. Stand in 75°F. (24°C.). When starter is going well (about 24 hours normally) boil up the elderberries for 15 minutes in 2 pints of water. Strain over sugar, tartaric acid and nutrient tablet in plastic bucket. Allow to cool and add rose-hip syrup. Top up to about 7-pint mark, stir well and place in a gallon jar. When at 70–75°F. (21–24°C.) add yeast starter and the pectic enzyme. Ferment to dryness and rack into another jar, top up with water if necessary, and fit a bored cork plugged with cotton wool. Leave on the yeast for 5 months without racking. Then bottle. Wine should be drinkable about 8 weeks after bottling, but will improve for many months.

DRY RED TABLE WINE (Chianti type)

Ingredients:	*British*	*Metric*	*U.S.A*
Red grape concentrate	2 pints	1⅛ litre	2 pints

Plus 15 mg. Vitamin B1

1 level teaspoon ammonium phosphate
½ teaspoonful potassium phosphate
¼ teaspoonful magnesium sulphate
1 level teaspoonful pectic enzyme
Water to 1 gallon (4½ litres)
Chianti, Burgundy or Bordeaux yeast

The ingredients are mixed in a gallon jar, and the yeast is added and an air-lock fitted to the jar. Fermentation proceeds at around 75°F. (24°C.) and is normally complete in 2–3 weeks. At this point the wine is racked off the yeast sediment, is dosed with 1 Campden tablet per gallon and put through a filter bag. This is not filtering as such, more a very fine straining. A large filter bag is used, holding a gallon. About a pint of the wine is taken, and into it is added 1 teaspoonful of asbestos pulp and a tablespoonful of filtering powder. These are well mixed and the mixture poured into the filter bag. The rest of the wine is then added and allowed to filter through. When half a gallon has filtered through, this is returned to the bag and allowed to filter through once more. The whole process takes about 1 hour and the wine is then matured in a topped up jar fitted with a bored cork plugged with cotton wool. Due to its balance and the dosage of air given during the filtering process, this wine matures very fast. It is probably best drunk as a rough Chianti about two to three months after the end of fermentation. It will, of course, mature to a better wine after further time, but I always prefer it as a very good *vin ordinaire.*

DRY RED WINE (Claret type)

Ingredients:	British	Metric	U.S.A
Sloes	2½ lb.	1¼ kg.	2¼ lb.
Raisins	1 lb.	½ kg.	1 lb.
Red grape concentrate	¾ pint	400 mls.	¾ pint
Sugar	½ lb.	220 gm.	½ lb.

Plus 1 teaspoonful pectic enzyme
    1 teaspoonful ammonium phosphate
    3 mg. Vitamin B1
    Bordeaux yeast starter
    Water to 1 gallon (4½ litres)

Method: Pour 4 pints of boiling water over the raisins, sugar, and crushed sloes. When cool add the pectic enzyme, ammonium phosphate, Vitamin B1 and the yeast. Ferment on the pulp for 3 days, then strain off into a gallon jar. Add the grape concentrate and top up to 1 gallon with cold water. Ferment on under an airlock. When fermentation is complete, rack off into another jar, top up with water and fit a bored cork plugged with cotton wool. Mature for about 18 months, with rackings every 4 months, each time topping up with water. This is a slow maturing wine, which will hold its quality for several years.

DRY RED TABLE WINE (Chateau-Neuf-du-Pape-type)

(This is fuller bodied than the previous red table wines.)

Ingredients:	British	Metric	U.S.A
Dried bilberries	¼ lb.	112 gm.	¼ lb.
Red grape concentrate	1 pint	½ litre	1 pint
Bananas	2 lb.	1 kg.	1½ lb.
Sugar	1 lb.	½ kg.	¾ lb.

Plus 1 teaspoonful pectic enzyme
    1 teaspoonful ammonium phosphate
    1 Vitamin B1 tablet (3 mg.)
    2 level teaspoonsful tartaric acid
    Burgundy yeast
Advisable ⅛ oz. succinic acid (3 gm.) if maturing for at
    least 1 year

Method: Peel the bananas, discarding the skins, and boil them for half an hour in 4 pints of water (2 litres). Strain the liquor over the bilberries and sugar, stir to dissolve and allow to cool.

Add the remaining ingredients, top up to 1 gallon and ferment for 5 days, stirring the pulp beneath the surface but keeping the plastic bucket covered meanwhile. Strain off the bilberries and continue fermentation under an air-lock in a gallon jar.

When fermentation is complete, first rack off the top half of the gallon jar, keeping the siphon tube half-way up the jar. Lightly filter the second half of the jar with a filter bag. One teaspoonful of asbestos pulp and a tablespoonful of filtering powder are added to the second half of the jar, the jar is thoroughly stirred and then poured into the filter bag. The wine will need to go through the bag twice, and then is added to the second jar which is topped up with water, fitted with a bored cork, plugged with cotton wool, and allowed to mature without any further racking for at least six months.

The purpose of this process is to retain the yeast floating in the top half of the fermentation jar and to remove the banana and other pulp in the bottom half. This then allows the finished wine to rest on pure yeast, which for certain types of wine is extremely beneficial.   •

The wine can be drunk after about three months, but is at its best after 18 months. If it is intended to mature it this long, a racking after 8 months and again at one year is advisable, with topping-up if necessary.

Sweet red wines

TARRAGONA TYPE WINE

Ingredients:	British	Metric	U.S.A
Sloes	3 lb.	1½ kg.	2½ lb.
Bananas	2 lb.	1 kg.	1½ lb.
Red grape concentrate	1 pint	½ litre	1 pint

Plus additives as above
    Sugar as required
    Port yeast starter
    Water to 1 gallon (4½ litres)

Method: First make the yeast starter by taking a clean sterile bottle and filling it up to the shoulder with a mixture of 1 part grape concentrate and 3 parts cold water. Add the yeast and plug the bottle with cotton wool. Place in a warm place (around 75°F. (24°C.)).

When the starter bottle is actively fermenting, commence preparation of the main brew. Peel the bananas and, discarding the skins, cut them into slices and boil with about 4 pints of water for half an hour. Then strain the banana liquor over the sloes in a plastic bucket. When cool add the grape concentrate and the additives. Stir well and finally (at about 75°F. (24°C.)) add the yeast starter bottle and cover the bucket. Ferment on the sloes for up to 5 days. The bucket should be inspected twice a day and the sloes crushed against the side of the bucket with a wooden spoon, and the bucket re-covered. Then strain the fermenting must into a gallon jar.

Meanwhile make a heavy syrup from 2 lb. sugar and 1 pint water boiled together (1 kg. in ½ litre water) and store it. Whenever the gravity falls to 10 add ¼ pint of syrup (say 140 mls.) and stir it in. For those not using a hydrometer, this is when the brew starts to taste dry. Continue this process until such time as an addition of syrup takes about 10 days to be absorbed. It is probable that more than a gallon of must will have been achieved, and the surplus is allowed to ferment out in a bottle plugged with cotton wool. Finally rack the wine into another jar, top up with wine and leave to mature, with rackings each 4 months.

MARSALA TYPE WINE

Ingredients:	British	Metric	U.S.A
Red cherries	6 lb.	3 kg.	5 lb.
Bananas	1 lb.	½ kg.	¾ lb.
Red grape concentrate	1 pint	½ litre	1 pint
Additives as above			
Marsala or port yeast			
Water to 1 gallon (4½ litres)			

Method: As for Tarragona type wine, except that the cherries should be crushed before pouring the banana liquor over them.

THE ENGLISHMAN'S PORT

Ingredients:	British	Metric	U.S.A
Bilberries	3 lb.	1½ kg.	2½ lb.
Bananas	2 lb.	1 kg.	1½ lb.
Red grape concentrate	1 pint	½ litre	1 pint
Additives as above			
1 teaspoonful tartaric acid			
Port yeast			
Water to 1 gallon (4½ litres)			

Method: As for Tarragona type.

AUTUMN SWEET

Ingredients:	*British*	*Metric*	*U.S.A*
Elderberries	2 lb.	1 kg.	1½ lb.
Red plums or bullaces	4 lb.	2 kg.	3 lb.
Bananas	1 lb.	½ kg.	1 lb.
Red grape concentrate	1 pint	½ litre	¾ pint

Additives and yeast as for Tarragona type

Method: As for Tarragona type, except that plums should be stoned before pouring banana liquor over them.

SWEET ELDERBERRY

Ingredients:	*British*	*Metric*	*U.S.A*
Elderberries	4 lb.	2 kg.	3 lb.
Bananas	2 lb.	1 kg.	1½ lb.
Red grape concentrate	½ pint	300 mls.	½ pint

Additives as above

1 teaspoonful tartaric acid

Madeira yeast

Water to 1 gallon (4½ litres)

Note: In all these sweet red wines there is enough acid present to maintain a sound fermentation. There may not be enough acid present in the final wine to balance the residual sugar content, especially if further sweetening is practised. This is due to climatic variance, and so test to see if a small addition of tartaric or malic acid improves the flavour. Probably the maximum ever needed would be 1 level teaspoonful of either.

DRY WHITE TABLE WINE (Moselle type)

Ingredients:	British	Metric	U.S.A
Green gooseberries	6 lb.	3 kg.	4½ lb.
White grape concentrate	1 pint	½ litre	1 pint
Honey	1 lb.	½ kg.	¾ lb.

Plus 1 teaspoonful ammonium phosphate
    1 teaspoonful pectic enzyme
    1 Vitamin B1 tablet (3 mg.)
    Bernkastler yeast
    Water to 1 gallon (4½ litres)

Method: Top and tail the gooseberries and pour 4 pints (2 litres) of boiling water over them. When cool, crush the fruit, add the remaining ingredients and top up to 1 gallon with cold water. Stir well to dissolve honey and add yeast. Ferment on the pulp for four days, then strain off the gooseberries. The acidity should ideally be tested at this point, due to the variances in the acidity of the gooseberries. The ideal acidity is about 4.8 p.p.t. (sulphuric) or about 7.0 p.p.t. in terms of tartaric acid (U.S.A. measurement). If it is higher than this, chalk can be added up to ¼ oz. per gallon, this reduces the acidity by about 1.7 p.p.t. (2.7 p.p.t. U.S.A.) using tartaric measurement. If more acid is required then malic acid *must* be used.

Ferment on in a gallon jar under an air-lock and at the end of fermentation add 1 Campden tablet and rack into another jar, top up with water and fit a bored cork plugged with cotton wool. If a heavy deposit forms within a fortnight, rack again and add another Campden tablet. Thereafter maturing should continue for a few months, but frequently this wine can be drunk with pleasure after only 8 weeks. Under these conditions it is frequently slightly *petillant* or sparkling.

DRY WHITE TABLE WINE (White Burgundy type)

Ingredients:	British	Metric	U.S.A
Peaches	6 lb.	3 kg.	5 lb.
White grape concentrate	½ pint	300 mls.	½ pint
Sugar	1 lb.	½ kg.	¾ kg.
Tartaric acid	¼ oz.	7 gm.	¼ oz.

Plus 1 teaspoonful pectic enzyme
1 teaspoonful ammonium phosphate
Burgundy yeast
Water to 1 gallon (4½ litres)

Method: Stone the peaches and press out the juice. Pour two pints of *cold* water over the peach pulp and press out the remaining juice. Add the grape concentrate, sugar, acid, pectic enzyme and ammonium phosphate, top up to 1 gallon and add 2 Campden tablets (100 p.p.m. sulphite). but before doing this take out about a cupful of juice, place in a clean bottle and add the yeast. Plug the bottle with cotton wool and place in a warm place (75°F. (24°C.)). After 36 hours add the yeast starter to the must and ferment in a gallon jar under an air-lock to completion.

When fermentation is complete, add 1 Campden tablet and rack into a second jar 3 days later. Top up with water and fit a bored cork plugged with cotton wool. Mature for at least 6 months with one racking at about 4 months (with topping up and a Campden tablet).

A faint residual sweetness will occur due to glycerol being formed from the initial sulphite. A great many people, in fact, like and drink this wine as a medium sweet wine, and for this purpose glycerol or glycerine is useful. When bottling, 1 fl. oz. per bottle (28 mls.) should be added. Do not exceed this dosage as the glycerine will otherwise add its own flavour to that of the wine.

LIPHOOK HOCK

This recipe originated as a beginner's wine but was then adapted and improved upon by various winemakers until it has become a standard good wine of the Amateur Winemaker movement.

Ingredients:	*British*	*Metric*	*U.S.A*
White grapes	1 lb.	450 gm.	¾ lb.
Raisins	1 lb.	450 gm.	¾ lb.
Split maize	½ lb.	225 gm.	½ lb.
Sugar	3 lb.	1½ kilos	2½ lb.

Plus 2 oranges
    2 lemons
    6 small potatoes
    2 apples
    Steinberg yeast
    Yeast nutrient
    Pectic destroying enzyme
    Water to 1 gallon (4½ litres)

Method: Make up a yeast starter bottle about 48 hours before making the wine. Use the juice of the oranges and lemons, 1 tablespoonful sugar, 1 tablespoonful malt extract, yeast, nutrient and a cupful of water. Place in a clean bottle and stand in a warm place until it is fermenting. Mince the potatoes, apples, grapes and raisins into a polythene bucket, add the sugar and maize, and ¾ gallon of boiling water. Stir to dissolve the sugar. When cool add the contents of the starter bottle, the pectic enzyme, then cover with a cloth. Keep at about 65–70°F. (18–24°C.) for at least 2 weeks, stirring twice daily. Then strain the liquor into a fermenting jar and make up to 1 gallon with cold boiled water. Allow to ferment until dry, then rack and add 1 Campden tablet. Store in a cool temperature (50°F. (10°C.)) if possible and keep for at least a year. A deposit will form again in the bottom of the container, but the wine can then be siphoned off into clean bottles.

DRY WHITE TABLE WINE (Graves type)

Ingredients:	British	Metric	U.S.A
Dessert apples	8 lb.	4 kg.	6½ lb.
White grape concentrate	1 pint	½ litre	¾ pint
Sugar	1 lb.	½ kg.	¾ lb.

Plus 1 teaspoonful pectic enzyme
    1 teaspoonful ammonium phosphate
    ½ teaspoonful tartaric acid
    1 Vitamin B1 tablet (3 mg.)
    Bordeaux yeast
    Water to 1 gallon (4½ litres)

Method: Wash, chop and press the apples, using a press or a liquidiser. The use of Rohament P (obtainable from winemaking suppliers) will increase the yield of juice. Add 2 Campden tablets to the juice and leave overnight. Strain off the juice from any pulp, add the remaining ingredients, top up to 1 gallon and ferment in a gallon jar under an air-lock. When fermentation is complete, rack off into another jar, add 1 Campden tablet and top up with water. Fit a bored cork plugged with cotton wool. Rack the wine at 3-monthly intervals, with topping up and with the addition of a Campden tablet, and the wine should be fit for drinking after about 6–9 months, although it will improve for up to 2 years.

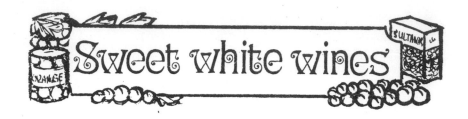

SWEET WHITE WINE (Sauternes type)

Sauternes obtains part of its silky smooth quality from an attack on the grapes of Botrytis Cinerea, a mould also known as Noble Rot. We can produce much the same result by a little game called "Bending the Krebs Cycle". An overdose of sulphite is given to the must, and a powerful yeast then destroys this before going on with the process of normal fermentation. This causes glycerol or glycerine to be formed in a natural way which simulates the original Sauternes model.

Ingredients:	*British*	*Metric*	*U.S.A*
Yellow plums	**3 lb.**	**1½ kg.**	**2½ lb.**
Bananas	**3 lb.**	**1½ kg.**	**2½ lb.**
White grape concentrate	**1 pint**	**½ litre**	**1 pint**
Tartaric acid	**½ oz.**	**14 gm.**	**½ oz.**
Malic acid	**¼ oz.**	**7 gm.**	**¼ oz.**
Sugar	**1½ lb.**	**750 gm.**	**1¼ lb.**

Plus 15 mg. Vitamin B1
    1 teaspoonful Ammonium phosphate
    Sauternes yeast
    Water to 1 gallon (4½ litres)

Method: First prepare the yeast starter by taking a clean wine bottle and filling it with ¼ grape concentrate and ¾ water. Mix well, add yeast and plug bottle with cotton wool. Stand in a warm place around 75°F. (24°C.). Meanwhile, peel the bananas, reject the skins, and boil the banana slices in 4 pints water (about 2 litres) for half an hour. Strain the hot liquor over the stoned plums, and when cool add the grape concentrate, acids, sugar and nutrients. Now add 4 Campden tablets (200 p.p.m. sulphite). Cover bucket. After 48 hours add the yeast starter and keep bucket covered, but stirring pulp beneath the surface once a day. It is probable that no activity will be observed for several days. After 5 days strain off the plums and continue in a gallon jar. By this time fermentation should be proceeding sluggishly and will gradually gain speed. When fermentation is complete, rack into another jar, top up with water, add 1 Campden tablet and fit a bored cork plugged with cotton wool. Mature for about 9 months with one intermediate racking, then sweeten up to desired taste. This wine matures at about 18 months. One example based on the above won two first prizes at London regional shows with an interval of two years between entries. It therefore holds its quality for a considerable time.

SWEET WHITE WINE (Tokay type)

Although these days we can simulate almost any commercial wine, Imperial Tokay is one of the few remaining unconquered peaks. It is so magnificent a wine that it virtually just stands there laughing at our efforts to match it. The following recipe is about the nearest that we have yet managed to approach it. It is a prize-winning wine, but it only has the slenderest hint of Tokay.

Ingredients:	*British*	*Metric*	*U.S.A*
Sultanas	2 lb.	1 kg.	1½ lb.
White grape concentrate	1 pint	½ litre	1 pint
Sugar	2 lb.	1 kg.	1½ lb.
Glycerol or glycerine	1½ fl. oz.	40 mls.	1½ fl. oz.
Tartaric acid	¼ oz.	7 gm.	¼ oz.
Malid acid	¼ oz.	7 gm.	¼ oz.

Plus 1 teaspoonful pectic enzyme
     15 mg. Vitamin B1
     1 teaspoonful ammonium phosphate
     Sauternes or Tokay yeast
     Water to 1 gallon (4½ litres)

Note. For reasons which I do not fully understand, certain Tokay musts are fermented at very high temperatures—around 90°F. (32°C.) even. Presumably it causes a certain "cooked" flavour which blends in during maturing to form part of the distinctive Tokay taste. Certain Californian wines have this flavour though achieved in a different manner. The experiment can be tried with a genuine Tokay yeast, but otherwise normal fermentation temperatures around 70°F. (21°C.) should be observed.

Method: Mince the sultanas and place in a plastic bucket with the other ingredients and water. Stir well and dissolve sugar and add 1 Campden tablet. Cover and leave for 24 hours. Then add yeast and ferment on the pulp for 4 days. Strain off into a gallon jar and continue fermentation. When fermentation is complete, rack off into a second jar, top up with water and fit a bored cork, plugged with cotton wool. Mature for 4 months, then rack again and sweeten up to taste. Leave for a further period—preferably a year—before drinking.

MIDDLESEX ORANGE TOKAY
This is a medium sweet sound wine designed to mature quickly and can be drunk within 6 months of bottling, although 1 year is recommended.

Ingredients:	*British*	*Metric*	*U.S.A*
Orange juice	2 pints	1⅛ litre	2 pints
White grape concentrate	1 pint	½ litre	1 pint
Sugar	3 lb.	1½ kilos	2½ lb.

Plus 1 nutrient tablet
    2 Vitamin B1 tablets (Benerva—3 mg. size)
    Tokay yeast
    Water to 1 gallon (4½ litres)

Method: Pour the orange juice into a gallon jar, add sugar and nutrients and 3 pints water. Add Tokay yeast and ferment for 1½ weeks at 70°–75°F. (21°–24°C.). At this point add the pint of grape concentrate, stir well to dissolve and ferment the wine to completion. It is an advantage to increase the temperature to 80°F. (27°C.) during the late stages of fermentation. While fermentation is proceeding, extract the zest from the thinly pared peel of 3 oranges with approximately ½ cup of vodka or brandy. When fermentation is complete rack the wine into a fresh jar and add the peel-flavoured spirit to the wine. Top up if necessary with water, and mature for at least 6 months.

PEACH AND RAISIN WINE

This recipe, originally printed in *'Amateur Winemaker'* is repeated since it was a prizewinner for Mr. Harold Cox.

Ingredients:	British	Metric	U.S.A
Peach slices	1½ lb.	700 gm.	1½ lb.
Raisins	1 lb.	450 gm.	¾ lb.
White grape concentrate	1 pint	½ litre	1 pint
Sugar	2 lb.	1 kilo	1¾ lb.

Plus ½ teaspoonful tannin
Pectic destroying enzyme
Yeast nutrients—1 tablet or 1 teaspoon ammonium
   phosphate
Sherry yeast
Water to 1 gallon (4½ litres)

Method: Mince raisins and pour on them about 3 pints of boiling water. When cool add peach pulp, grape concentrate, pectic enzyme, nutrient and yeast. Ferment on the pulp for 5–7 days. Strain into a fermentation jar and add 1 lb. sugar (½ kilo) (in syrup form). After a further 7 days, add another pound of sugar and add grape tannin and top up with cool boiled water.

First rack when fermentation ends (3 weeks to 1 month according to the temperature of the room).

Rack again 4 weeks later. This leaves a good air space at the top of the fermentation jar, which should be plugged with cotton wool to allow oxidation and form a sherry type flavour. Leave for 5 to 6 months.

If kept at 45°–50°F. (7–13°C.) and the S.G. is 1000 or below, a sherry flor may form and so help to produce a fine sherry flavour. Rack for the third time. Bottle after 1 year. The finished wine is approximately 18% by volume or 31° proof, acidity 3.5.

Dessert wines

Dessert wines are, by and large, about 22% alcohol by volume or around 36 degrees proof—the strength of Port. Until recently these have been strong wines fortified further with Polish Spirit, and special classes have been allocated to them in regional and national shows. Science, however, moves on, and it is possible under ideal circumstances to produce such wines by direct fermentation, an idea which would have been considered quite impossible a few years back. Even so, the majority of our wines do not present the special circumstances required, so for this section only three recipes are given, one for a normal wine plus fortification and the second for the ideal balance with normal fermentation to achieve this gigantic amount of alcohol. The final one—Bilberry Port—is a considerable prize winner.

NORMAL WINE PLUS FORTIFICATION

Ingredients:	British	Metric	U.S.A
Apples	6 lb.	3 kg.	5 lb.
White grape concentrate	1 pint	½ litre	1 pint
Sugar (initially)	2 lb.	1 kg.	1½ lb.
Tartaric acid	¼ oz.	7 gm.	¼ oz.

Plus 1 teaspoonful pectic enzyme
    1 teaspoonful ammonium phosphate
    Vitamin B1 (15 mg.)
    ¼ teaspoonful grape tannin
Sauternes yeast
Water to 1 gallon (4½ litres)

Method: Chop the apples and place in a plastic bucket along with the other ingredients. Make up to 1 gallon with cold water and stir well to dissolve sugar. Add 1 Campden tablet, cover and add the yeast 24 hours later. Ferment on the pulp for 3 days then strain off the apples and continue fermentation in a gallon jar. Whenever

116

gravity falls to zero add ¼ lb. sugar in syrup form (about 100 gm.). This will cause the volume to exceed the gallon and the extra should be kept fermenting in a spare bottle and used to top up at racking time. When the wine will absorb no more sugar and is fermented out dry, rack into another jar, top up and add 1 Campden tablet.

The wine is then matured in the ordinary way with rackings at each 3 months (with topping up and a Campden tablet). When the wine is clear and somewhat matured, prepare for fortification.

Provided a wine is dry, not containing any sugar, a much maligned instrument, the vinometer, can be employed. This is a cheap device consisting of a small tulip bulb connected to a capillary tube. The bulb is filled with wine and it drips through the capillary. Then the tube is inverted and the level of wine noted on the tube. It is a device which will not work with sweet wines since the sugar will give readings far in excess of the alcohol content, and it will not work accurately for long unless it is kept in good condition. In order to keep a vinometer in good condition it is necessary to rinse it out with methylated spirits after each testing, and to keep it permanently in a bottle of methylated spirits. Under these conditions it will give quite a period of service with moderate accuracy with dry wines.

Having discovered with the vinometer how strong the wine is, the next question is how much fortifying spirit is required to be added in order to achieve a wine of dessert strength. This is done by means of Pearson's Square:

$$
\begin{array}{ccc}
A & & B \\
80 & & 15 \\
& C & \\
& 20 & \\
5 & & 60 \\
D & & E \\
\end{array}
$$

A is the alcoholic strength of the spirit   (% alcohol
B is the alcoholic strength of the wine   by volume)
C is the desired alcoholic strength
D equals $C-B$
E equals $A-C$

In the example given we have assumed we are fortifying with 140 proof Polish spirit (which is 80% by volume—you divide the proof figure by 4/7) and that the wine is 15% alcohol by volume—a normal top strength wine as determined by the vinometer. The desired strength is 20% by volume or 35 proof.

The figures 80 and 15 are entered at A and B and the desired strength 20 at C. The difference between A and C is entered at E and the difference between B and C is entered at D. The final figures D and E give the volume of spirit and wine needed to achieve 20% wine or 35 proof. Thus 5 volumes of 140 proof spirit are needed for every 60 volumes of wine, or 1 of spirit to 12 of wine. Thus 1 pint of 140 proof vodka mixed with 12 pints of wine will produce 13 pints of 35 proof wine.

Having fortified the wine, it will be necessary to adjust it for sugar and acid, and this must be done by taste. Sugar is dealt with first and then acid. The sugar addition will dilute the alcoholic strength and the winemaker can decide to settle for a dessert wine of around, say, 32 proof or add a little more Polish Spirit to restore the Port strength of the wine.

The wine now needs a further period of maturing in order that the blend of wine, spirit and sugar can be effected. A wine of this strength can of course be kept for perhaps twenty years with advantage.

DESSERT WINE BY DIRECT FERMENTATION

This involves producing a wine must of absolute balance and caring for it through all its stages. The basic ingredient is red grape concentrate (only the best will do) plus a range of nutrients. As the yeast becomes tolerant of the alcohol (and this needs the best yeast) the must is fed with a mixture of sugar syrup and more grape concentrate. Under these conditions, based on the experiments of about a dozen winemakers, it is possible to achieve between 19% and 22% alcohol by volume. This is 33—38 degrees proof, the lower end of which is quite sufficient for a dessert wine.

Ingredients:

	British	Metric	U.S.A
Best red grape concentrate	2 pints	1⅛ litre	2 pints

Plus 15 mg. Vitamin B1

    1 teaspoonful ammonium phosphate
    ½ teaspoonful potassium phosphate
    ¼ teaspoonful magnesium sulphate
    1 teaspoonful pectic enzyme
    Grey Owl Madeira yeast
    Water to 1 gallon (4½ litres)
    More grape concentrate needed for fortification process

Method: Place all the ingredients in a gallon jar and add water up to the 6 pint level (British), 4 litre mark (metric), or 5 pint level (U.S.A). Stir well to dissolve and add yeast. Ferment at 75°F. (24°C.).

Meanwhile make up a mixture of ½ pint grape concentrate, ½ lb. sugar and ¼ pint water. In metric this is around 300 mls. grape concentrate 100 gms. sugar and 150 mls. water. Stir well to dissolve.

During the first fortnight, whenever the gravity falls to 10 add ¼ pint of this mixture (about 150 mls.). After this period make this addition whenever the gravity falls to 5. When fermentation has been continuing for 1 month, try and increase the temperature to 80°F. (27°C.) and continue the process of additions. Fermentation normally continues for 8 to 9 weeks, and the fortification mixture above has to be repeated at least once. In rare cases it will be found that there is no more room in the jar, in which case about a pint has to be transferred into a bottle which is plugged with cotton wool and kept in the same temperature. When additions of the concentrated/sugar mixture only have to be made about once in 10 days, it can be considered that the wine is of the desired strength. A Campden tablet is added to the ferment and the wine is racked off 3 days later into a second jar and topped up with spare wine or with water.

At this stage you will have a powerful balanced wine of great bouquet flavour and vinosity which may however be over-acid. The next stage is to chill the wine, so that some of the excess tartaric acid crystallises out as cream of tartar. Ideally this is done by putting the jar out in the cold on a winter's night or two and pouring the wine away from the crystals forming at the bottom of the jar. It can of course be done in the refrigerator by using plastic containers and putting the wine in the deep freeze part for some hours. Normally the wine will not freeze under these conditions due to its strength and only crystal formation will occur.

Where it is found that chilling fails to produce cream of tartar crystals, an addition of ¼ oz. (7 gm.) Precipitated Chalk (calcium carbonate) should be added to neutralise part of the acid, and the wine be allowed to rest for 10 days before being racked to remove sediment.

The final stage is to sweeten the wine up to Port standard. In order to so this a heavy syrup is made from 2 lb. sugar and 1 pint water boiled together (1 kg. sugar with ½ litre of water). About 1 part of this syrup with 5 parts of wine is approximately the mixture, but the final dosage should be made by tasting. The important thing is to add enough sugar so that the acid taste remaining seems to be balanced by the sugar. Once this has been done, the wine is stored away for some months to mature and blend. It can then be bottled and drunk after, say, six months, but will improve for several years. It will hold its excellence for perhaps a generation. It is the sort of wine one makes when a child is born, for its twenty-first birthday.

BILBERRY PORT
(Winner of several first prizes)

Ingredients:	British	Metric	U.S.A
Red grape concentrate	**1 pint**	**½ litre**	**1 pint**
Bananas	**2 lb.**	**1 kg.**	**2 lb.**
Bilberries	**4 lb.**	**2 kg.**	**4 lb.**

(These can be replaced by one-quarter of their weight of dried Bilberries)
Plus 1 teaspoonful ammonium phosphate or a nutrient tablet
    1 level teaspoonful tartaric acid
    1 teaspoonful pectinol, or pectolase
    Madeira or port yeast
    Sugar as required
    Water to 1 gallon (4½ litres)

Method: First make yeast starter in a wine bottle using 1 dessert-spoonful of grape concentrate, 1 dessertspoonful sugar, half a nutrient tablet and half a teaspoonful of citric acid. Top up to shoulder of bottle with water, shake to dissolve and add yeast.

When starter is active, boil up the bananas wth their skins in 3 pints of water for half an hour and strain liquor over 1 lb. (½ kg.) of sugar in a plastic bucket. Stir to dissolve, and add bilberries. When cool add grape concentrate and top up with water to about 7-pint level. Add yeast starter and pectic enzyme when temperature is between 70°–75°F. (21–24°C.).

Cover bucket and ferment on pulp for 4 days, then strain off into a gallon jar and fit an airlock. Meantime make up a heavy sugar syrup by boiling up 2 lb. sugar with 1 pint of water (1 kg. with ½ litre). For the first fortnight in the jar test the gravity of the must every few days and when it falls below 10 add ¼ pint of sugar syrup (150 mls.) Then let the gravity fall down to zero and again add ¼ pint of syrup. Continue adding ¼ pints of syrup whenever the zero mark is reached until you find there is about a 10-day gap between additions. The wine can then be racked off into another jar, given a dose of 2 Campden tablets, and the jar topped up with water. If a heavy deposit forms within the next fortnight, rack the wine once more to remove it. Thereafter rack at 3-monthly intervals.

This wine requires about 18 months to mature, but will be a powerful full bodied clear red wine of about 18% alcohol.

When wine is mature it requires sweetening and this should be done with either bilberry juice, Ribena, or red grape concentrate. About half a pint of this will be needed, and should be added in stages with small tastings in between. Allow a further short period to complete the blending.

Sherry starts out life as an ordinary white wine, but it is exposed to the air in containers which are not full during maturing. Some of these sherries become oxidised and are then sweetened to form what is known as Oloroso sherry. Others, however, develop a thick yeast film on the surface known as a "flor" and this produces a similar but finer flavour. These are kept as dry sherries or Finos. The first recipe for Dry Fino sherry is a bit special for by balancing a must to the chemical constituents of a sherry must I managed to achieve this phenomenon of a sherry flor on a mixture of fruit. I used a Grey Owl Sherry yeast, and Mrs. Suzanne Tritton of Grey Owl laboratories assisted greatly in establishing that it was a genuine sherry flor, the first one recorded in Britain, using mixed fruits.

DRY FINO SHERRY

Ingredients:	*British*	*Metric*	*U.S.A*
Bananas	1 lb.	½ kg.	¾ lb.
Apples	2 lb.	1 kg.	1½ lb.
Gypsum	1 oz.	28 gm.	1 oz.
White grape concentrate	1 pint	½ litre	1 pint
Cream of tartar	½ oz.	14 gm.	½ oz.
Pectic enzyme	¼ oz.	7 gm.	¼ oz.
Tannic acid	1/20th oz.	1 gm.	1/20th oz.
Ammonium phosphate	1/7th oz.	4 gm.	1/7th oz.

Plus Sugar—1¼ lb. boiled up with ¾ pint water and stored for use as described (500 gm. with 400 mls. water)
Grey Owl Sherry yeast
Water to 1 gallon (4½ litres)

Method: Boil the bananas, including skins, in 4 pints (2 litres) of water for half an hour. Meanwhile core apples, chop and place in a polythene bucket. Strain liquor from bananas over apples. Add grape concentrate. Cover bucket with blanket and allow to cool. When cool add cream of tartar, gypsum, pectic enzyme, tannic acid, ammonium phosphate and yeast starter. Stir twice daily, keeping well covered in between, and after 3 days strain off the apples and continue fermentation. Add the remaining sugar syrup from this point on at a rate of ¼ pint per day (142 mls.) until all has been absorbed, then top up with water to 1 gallon (4½ litres).

When fermentation is complete siphon off (rack) into a container big enough to allow a fair air space above the wine and plug with cotton wool. This racking is the only one in sherry making, and it is important that pulp debris does not get sucked into the new container. If by any chance this does occur it is best to do a second racking about 2 weeks later in order to remove this pulp.

Leave the jar in a cool place (50°–60°F., 10°–16°C.), and do not disturb. A flor may form on the surface in a few weeks or months. The jar must then be left until all the flor has finally sunk to the bottom, after which the wine can be bottled. If a flor does not form (as should be the case for sweet Oloroso type sherries) the wine can be sweetened with white grape concentrate or sugar syrup shortly before bottling unless the winemaker prefers to leave it dry. A raisin extract prepared by boiling 1 lb. raisins (450 gm.) in 2 pints of water (1⅛ litre) for half an hour, carefully straining off the pulp and evaporating the extract to about half its original volume, can also be used for sweetening.

ALTERNATIVES FOR DRY SHERRIES

The following fruits, etc., are to replace the Apples and Bananas in the preceding Dry Fino recipe. All other ingredients are as before.

	British	Metric	U.S.A
1. **Raisins**	4 lb.	2 kg.	3¼ lb.
2. **Peaches**	5 lb.	2½ kg.	4 lb.
3. **Yellow plums**	3 lb.	1½ kg.	2½ lb.
4. **Bananas**	2 lb.	1 kg.	1½ lb.
5. **Parsnips**	4 lb.	2 kg.	3¼ lb.

In this recipe, the parsnips are sliced and boiled in an open pan for half an hour, and the liquor allowed to cool and settle before being added to other ingredients.

```
┌────────────────────────────────────────────────────────────┐
│   BASIC ADDITIVES FOR 1 GALLON                              │
│                                                             │
│   15 mg. Vitamin B1                                         │
│   1 teaspoonful ammonium phosphate                          │
│   2 heaped teaspoonfuls tartaric acid                       │
│   1 level teaspoonful pectic enzyme                         │
└────────────────────────────────────────────────────────────┘
```

SWEET OLOROSO SHERRY

Only two recipes are given for this, but both have been used with success on several occasions by myself.

Ingredients:	British	Metric	U.S.A
Parsnips	4 lb.	2 kg.	3¼ lb.
Bananas	1 lb.	½ kg.	¾ lb.
White grape concentrate	1 pint	½ litre	1 pint

Additives as above
Sugar as required
Water to 1 gallon
Sherry yeast

Method: Scrub the parsnips and cut into slices. Peel the bananas and throw away the skins. Boil the parsnip and banana slices in about 4 pints water (say 2 litres) for half an hour, then strain the liquid over 2 lb. sugar (1 kg.) in a plastic bucket. When cool, add the grape concentrate and additives. Make up to the 7 pint mark with cold water (4 litres metric, 6 pint mark U.S.A.), and ferment in the bucket for a few days. Then strain through a nylon sieve into a gallon jar to remove small pieces of pulp and continue fermentation under an air-lock.

Make up a sugar solution by boiling 2 lb. sugar with 1 pint water (1 kg. with ½ litre water) and store this for use. When ever the gravity of the must has dropped to 10 (or the wine tastes fairly lacking in sugar) add ¼ pint of the sugar solution to the fermenting must (about 150 mls.). Continue to do this until such an addition is only required after an interval of 10 days.

Allow the must to ferment out, then rack into a second jar top up with spare wine if necessary, fit a bored cork plugged with cotton wool and leave for two weeks. Rack once more into jars but this time only fill the jar about two-thirds with the wine. Again fit a bored cork plugged with cotton wool, or simply plug the top of the jar with a large plug of cotton wool. Place in a cool place. The wine should be tasted about once a month to find the point at which sufficient sherry flavour has been obtained. This will vary slightly from wine to wine, but normally about three or four months oxidation will be sufficient.

. If at this point the wine is not clear, transfer it into another jar and top up the jar with wine and/or sugar syrup—i.e. start the sweetening process. The amount of sugar required depends on your own palate. Further sweetening can be done when the wine is clear, matured and ready for bottling.

SECOND VARIATION SWEET SHERRY

Ingredients:	British	Metric	U.S.A
Yellow plums	3 lb.	1½ kg.	2½ lb.
Bananas	2 lb.	1 kg.	1½ lb.
White grape concentrate	1 pint	½ litre	1 pint

Additives as for first recipe, but reduce the tartaric acid to 1 heaped teaspoonful

Method: Boil the sliced bananas for half an hour, as before, and strain the liquor over the stoned plums and sugar in the plastic bucket. Then add the remaining ingredients, when cool, and proceed as before.

INDEX

INDEX

INDEX

INDEX

INDEX

INDEX

NOTES